confessions
from an
honest wife

confessions
from an
honest wife

on the mess,
mystery & miracle
of marriage

sarah zacharias davis

Revell

Grand Rapids, Michigan

© 2006 by Sarah Zacharias Davis

Published by Fleming H. Revell
a division of Baker Publishing Group
P.O. Box 6287, Grand Rapids, MI 49516-6287
www.revellbooks.com

Printed in the United States of America

Library of Congress Cataloging-in-Publication Data
Davis, Sarah Zacharias, 1975–
    Confessions from an honest wife : on the mess, mystery, and miracle of
marriage / Sarah Zacharias Davis.
        p.   cm.
    Includes bibliographical references.
    ISBN 10: 0-8007-3091-7 (pbk.)
    ISBN 978-0-8007-3091-8 (pbk.)
    1. Christian women—Religious life. 2. Married women—Religious life.
3. Wives—Religious life. 4. Marriage—Religious life—Christianity.
I. Title.
BV4528.15.D39 2006
248.8′435—dc22   2005033789

For Naomi, with whom I can always be real.
For Grace, who first showed me how.
And for Jeremy, who loves me in spite of it.

contents

The Mess and Mystery of Marriage

introductory thoughts on expectations versus realities

The young woman shields her face from the sun and looks both ways before crossing the street. She walks briskly toward the restaurant as she catches sight of her friend waiting at the door. Unconsciously, she adjusts the ring between her fingers, spinning it around, not entirely used to the feel of the cold metal of her not-yet-sized wedding band. Then she stops herself and waves at her friend. They embrace.

"How's married life?" her friend asks, smiling.

"Absolutely wonderful," she answers without thought or hesitation.

And maybe it really is. Maybe it's what she always thought it would be. Maybe she's as exuberantly happy as she appears. But if she were a little confused, a little disappointed, maybe not quite as happy as she expected, would she admit it?

The two women enjoy lunch together, sipping iced tea, tasting fresh salads, animatedly chatting. They're friends. But the layers are never peeled away to expose the interior beneath.

Across town, a group of women gather in a home for a weekly Bible study. They arrive in a steady stream, Bibles and notebooks in hand, most a few minutes late and effusing apologies and excuses of children and schedules. The evening is spent in laughter, thought, discussion. They joke, sometimes rolling their eyes at the events of their day and demands of their children, jobs, mothers, and pets. Most of the conversation inevitably turns to their husbands and marriages—marriage is something they all have in common.

Though they delve into the study, a study of a faith and a Creator who knows each one of them intimately, each woman maintains an invisible wall shielding her from the others. Each woman shares only what she feels will be orthodox with the others in the group.

Many women long for more, but no one's willing to chisel away the first brick.

When I was in college I was part of a Bible study group that was comprised of girls around my age, all of whom lived in close proximity to me. I cannot at all remember what we were studying or really any of what we discussed, with one exception. One of my dearest friends made a casual statement about something she was in a habit of doing, and she felt it was a weakness. It wasn't an earth-shattering revelation; there wasn't a whole lot of drama to the confession, it was just part of her life, and we moved on. But I was stuck there. Because, for one, it was something I struggled with as well. But it wasn't only that. I was struck by the fact that though I could have, I would never have admitted that weakness. I asked myself why. Did I think less of her for having learned about her fault? No, on the contrary, I felt closer to her and now held her in higher respect than just a few minutes before. Why couldn't I be honest about my weaknesses and, yes, sinfulness? Why did I have to pretend to be perfect and have it all together when that was far from the case?

Skip ahead to years later. It was just after my honeymoon, and I'd returned to work. A girl I casually knew stopped by my cube to welcome me back. She asked me how married life was. I said it was great (of course). She tilted her head to the side as if to get a better look at me and said, "Is it really?" I was immediately uncomfortable under the scrutiny, and before I could respond again she said, "Because you can say if it isn't what you expected. I have a friend who got married and found it really difficult, but she never felt like she could tell people." She waited for my response. I responded by saying it really was fine, and she shrugged and walked away. Would I have told her if there were anything that had disappointed me? No way! And that may be okay, because I barely knew her, but the truth is I would never have told even those closest to me. I won't even answer the question "What is the one body part you would change on yourself?" because I'm afraid to point out a flaw that someone may not have noticed and then draw attention to it. It's silly, yes, but it's more than that. Because at times in my life I have learned life-changing things. I have become the person I am, in part, through my experiences, having gained the limps, the epiphanies, and the acceptance that comes through those happenings. And if I can't be honest about who that person is, then what's the use? If I can't really touch another life and have their life touch mine, then what's the point of us all being here together? What are families, friendships, communities, and churches for?

Why is it we so often don't share our deepest thoughts and angst? Why do so many of us feel the need to project an image of perfection, beauty, of having it all together? Why is it so necessary to project spiritual strength and happiness—is this really for the benefit or detriment of other women?

In the movie *Miss Congeniality*, which satirizes the world of beauty pageants, Miss Texas makes it very clear that she won't put anything in her mouth that's not leafy and green. She even makes jokes about purging. Yet when she makes her presentation in the pageant in front of thousands of people, Miss Texas claims to eat all the Mexican food she can get her hands on. What she really means is "I look beautiful and thin, and it takes no effort or sacrifice on my part." At least that's what she wants others to think. But what's so wrong with a person who has to work at staying healthy and fit rather than just naturally being that way?

What's wrong is that this makes Miss Texas human. It makes her like most other people who have to work to look a certain way, rather than just being born beautiful. Some would call that ordinary, and who wants to be ordinary?

So these are the games women play with women.

There are others. Take shoes, for example.

I heard someone recently say on a morning talk show that sometimes we dress for men and sometimes for women, meaning that many outfits aren't equally appreciated by both genders. Shoes, for instance, are for women. (Shoes are my personal passion—and after I receive my credit card statement each month, they're my vice as well.) After all, how many average men do you know who compliment a woman on her shoes? So women mostly wear different shoes to impress other *women*. With numerous styles—from classy to sexy or funky—shoes allow a woman to portray any image she wants, and make any kind of statement she's in the mood to personify.

See how we play these games? Even as Christians we play them. We seem so fearful of showing weakness. But why? Ours is a faith based on the gift of grace, yet we fear grace will not be shown to us if we reveal our true selves. Perhaps this fear is, in part, because we've not shown grace to others.

At year-end, Christmas cards to friends, families, and business acquaintances show glossy photos of perfect families accompanied by a chronicle of the year's successes and accomplishments from Dad to the family pet. Most never tout the disappointments or heartaches, though for your average family the year would have been filled with both. We've all been guilty of it. We fudge on everything from weight and age to cosmetic surgery, troubled children, what we deem as personal failure, and how God speaks to us personally.

For one thing, we're not honest with one another about marriage. A friend of mine, for example, recently looked for three couples whose marriages would be worth emulating, couples who could dispense advice at the wedding of her son.

She struggled to find just three.

Though most couples would claim love as the reason they married—and indeed that is the most desirable reason—others admit (not as easily) to "lesser" reasons: cultural pressure, guilt, boredom, lack of fulfillment, loneliness.

13

The Cowboy Junkies song "Misguided Angel" tells of one such story. A woman, after the objections of each of her family members over the man she's chosen to be with, tells her well-meaning sister that she's tired of being alone night after night. She's tired of only dreaming of finding the right guy, and so she's going to marry this one anyway.

And yet . . .

Though we're in an age in which relative equality for women is enjoyed, and women can proudly choose not to marry, they *do* marry. And today's immense collection of love songs, romantic comedies, and romance novels reveals that the majority of women desire marriage. For good reason. God created marriage and declared it good.

But there are huge expectations for marriage.

History is filled with famous love stories, from the poetry and love letters exchanged between Elizabeth Barrett and Robert Browning in the mid-1800s, to C. S. Lewis's grief observed over losing his wife, Joy Davidman, in the 1950s, to Nancy Reagan's last embrace of Ronald Reagan.

I find myself unabashedly staring when I see elderly couples walking and holding hands, couples who have spent more of their lives together than apart. How much they must know about each other, how much they've experienced together, both painful and pleasurable. How vast the store of memories they've created together. These examples are real-life great loves, not Hollywood fabrications.

Don't we all desire a love so rich, so deep—an attainable dream that can be realized with true love, hard work, and great commitment? Could our own marriages be stronger if our expectations and the way we helped one another work through the realities were more real? What if we were honest with each other about marriage?

In the mid-sixties, some women tried. They came together in consciousness-raising or CR groups that by the 1970s grew into a movement in which thousands of women met together, one small group at a time, to identify with one another through their commonalities. Women in CR groups sought to better themselves, heal emotional anxieties like identity crises, and explore practical issues of womanhood. They met in their living rooms, breaking down social and racial barriers, and opened the lines of communication with one another, sharing a range of feelings: depression, fear, anger, uselessness, fulfillment, victory, and joy. Each woman was given freedom to share what was on her heart and mind, and share the women did—openly and honestly. (For many, the practical issues gave way to educating themselves as feminists, and later many groups became politically active in the movement as a result, but CR was not intended to be political and was never meant to launch a feminist movement.)

As a result, both comfort and empowerment were born of this camaraderie. With the number of women flocking to CR groups, the movement became one of the largest education and support vehicles for women this country has seen. And as a result, many of these women became instruments of change for their country, their communities, and even for their own families.

Imagine something similar happening in the lives of Christian women.

This book is not an invitation to CR. Nor is it about the games we play with women, men, the world, or the church.

No rules will be established and prescribed, no pat advice given or step-by-step formulas spelled out.

Instead you'll find just the truth of our lives, plain and unvarnished. The truth of expectations and realities of women of all ages, experiences, and stages of marriage—stories told candidly, intimately, as if you were talking with a trusted friend.

Victorian novelist George Eliot offered, "What greater thing is there for two human souls than to feel that they are joined for life; to strengthen each other in all labor, to rest on each other in all sorrow, to minister to each other in all pain, to be one with each other in silent, unspeakable memories at the moment of parting."[1] But G. K Chesterton said, on the contrary, that marriage is like an adventure, like going to war. Each evokes an entirely different thought and emotional impression.

Women in these pages explore how marriage can be both—still and steadfast one moment, fierce and robust the next, and always a wonderful mystery. These women explore how marriage is like (or not) the loves and unions in movies we've all seen—whether true love exists in a form so passionate that one would do anything, go anywhere, abandon everything just to be with that love; or whether love and marriage are simply that willingness to just do life together, or just intense infatuation grounded in insecurity and desperate dependence. These women talk about what real love is, whether fierce passion is sustainable, and what or who is a soul mate.

Even though I've penned every chapter, the accounts come from real interviews with real women, dealing with the issues of marriage. These are authentic women, many of whom have played the same games we all do. But believing in the purpose of this book, they have laid bare their souls in the spirit of true sisterhood so that we may learn, share, identify with, and be inspired by them. Some of the insights are theirs and some are mine, but the stories are true and real.

Their honesty will help reveal discoveries about not just love and marriage, but about life, what it means to be a woman, and what it means both to love and be loved by God.

The community of women in these pages have boldly risked authenticity. They've bared their hearts and souls. But make no mistake. Their confessions are not about men and how they've done us wrong. Rather, you'll see, many of the men discussed in these chapters are loving, giving men—men who are working just as hard as their wives to make this journey a lasting one.

But this is a book about us as women—real women, with all our complexities and our real marriages. This is a book about who we really are and where we believe we can go.

My hope for this book is that you find yourself somewhere among these pages in a kindred spirit of shared thoughts, feelings, questions, and answers. There is a common thread among all of us as women that binds us together.

And second, I hope that you'll learn more about yourself and the faith that shapes who you are and who you'll become as you tread this course you have chosen.

Lastly, it's my desire that we will all see and embrace the beauty and all that's gained in being real.

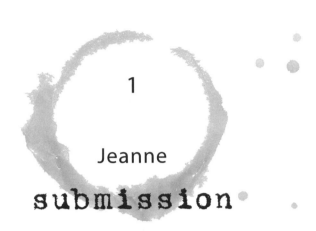

1

Jeanne

submission

Marriage is that relation between a man and woman in which the independence is equal, the dependence mutual, and the obligation reciprocal.

Louis Anspacher

I'm uncharacteristically carefree as I wander among the boutiques and little shops on a short break from my workday. I'm in search of just the right birthday gift, and the joy of this simple errand, combined with the warmth of this first spring day after months of cold, makes me feel happy to be alive. My skin, pale from winter, tingles at the sun's rays—a pleasant sensation, a distraction from the realities of the morning and the evening ahead.

Back in my car, beginning the ten-minute drive to my office, I feel as if I'm released from the hypnosis of the sun because I suddenly realize I've just spent forty-five minutes in easy thought and contentment. *How is it I could forget the rest of the world around me, all my responsibilities, and even temporarily abandon my usual internal discourse?*

That discourse is part of my tension these days—nagging thoughts about my decisions and choices, how I react and think.

You see, I'm not the person I used to be. What I once wanted out of life—where I wanted to go, what I wanted to be—has changed. Somewhere in the last ten years, I ceased to be the girl who just wanted to get married and have a family, who only wanted a job to pass the time before being a mom, and who chose her career based on those dreams. The combination of those things just isn't me anymore, and I don't really know that it ever was.

Now, some days, I feel that I must sacrifice everything I want, that parts of my life will remain an unfulfilled dream. On those days I feel suffocated. Marriage seems like an insurmountable uphill climb that never has a downhill on the other side. The compromises, the sacrifices baffle me. I often equate sacrifice with submission, and I've found the concept of submission opposite to what makes sense—fulfilling my needs in order to be a better wife, mother, helpmate, and friend. If I reject the idea of meeting my needs, I'm utterly mystified as to how I can live as a wife. Because when does compromising become compromising who you are, who you were meant to be, and—worse—when does it compromise your value as a woman, as a human being? Is there a distinguishing line?

This is the tension I deal with these days—a struggle to figure out what submission means in marriage and in everyday life.

Living this tension is exhausting, like a juggling act of try-ing to hold in check too many messages: what culture says, and experience—how I was raised by my parents—and the influence of my friends and church, and, most important, what I understand the Bible to say.

To understand this you have to understand that I was young, in my early twenties, when I got married. I thought I knew about marriage, the hard work, the compromise, the communication, all the stuff that everyone always talks about. It's positively cliché, but I thought I was mature and knew who I was. Besides, if marriage was all the hard work everyone said it was, I was ready. I was never one to be intimidated by hard work.

So my fiancé and I sailed through marriage counseling with ease, attending session after session and reading all the required books. I didn't feel as if I'd learned anything from all this that I hadn't already heard anyway. *Marriage is hard work. You have to compromise. We all have a love language. God is the third person in your marriage. Yada, yada, yada.*

I was as prepared as I could be.

Armed, then, with an arsenal of head knowledge and never a moment of hesitation, my husband and I took the proverbial plunge amid much fanfare.

I then braced myself for this jarring experience that everyone had predicted—the difficulty of adapting to what all the books said to expect in the first year of marriage. Like a child in a doctor's office with eyes scrunched tight, body rigid, waiting for the bite of the needle from a required booster shot, I was prepared for a shock.

And then . . . nothing. Nothing except peaceful partnership and easiness together.

Only, looking back, I believe that's when my questions on submission began to take root. Those early years of marriage with my husband were enjoyable enough. And so with confidence and ease I entered that time as one of self-exploration and growing up, learning who I really was, what I thought, and what I wanted for my life. I was unrestricted by my family's expectations or the pressure of friends, so I continued to mature and reinvent myself, as many twentysomethings do.

In the process, I accumulated more and more pictures of what a good marriage looked like to the church and to the world. Pictures, along with questions, began to build in my mind. *How does being a good wife by the world's standards fit with what I observed growing up in a-good, functional home? How does that fit with what the church says? What does a good wife look like in everyday life?*

I'd always taken for granted all the ideas about faith, the world, marriage, and being a wife, so I never really gave much thought to how all these things must blend together, how I would fit them into the marriage I'd helped create. And now the pictures seemed so opposite. *How do they fit? Which one is right?* I became bewildered and exhausted by all the uncertainty running through my head. I just couldn't quiet my mind. I felt as though I'd walked into a room, closed the door behind me, and now the space around me was shrinking smaller and smaller like some bizarre nightmare you have after eating too much before bed. I'd taken the plunge and now desperately needed air.

How could I not be overwhelmed and confused?

On one hand there was the world, the culture, telling me that I'm weak if I die to myself or sacrifice everything; that if I don't speak my mind, I'm spineless and unintelligent; that I'll lose myself and become unhappy unless I try to meet my own needs first so I can better meet the needs of those I love; and the world is open to my dreams and I can be a butterfly, airborne here and there as my heart desires.

Then on the other hand I had some Christians telling me that I should never question my husband's decisions, that God made man to rule over woman, and that I must respect my husband's decisions regardless of my own feelings. The implications followed: you don't need to think for yourself, and maybe you shouldn't because you must only follow. Your needs aren't as important. Never mind if you need to be intellectually stimulated and understood and encouraged to believe in your dreams. Your husband's needs are worthier. You should no longer work outside the home, because your calling is now in the home, and your occupation should be as a full-time wife, mother, housekeeper, and chef. Oh yeah, and you have to have sex with your husband whenever he wants it because you're not allowed to withhold. This is what unselfishness looks like. This is the picture of submissiveness. This is right.

Is it really right? Do "chefs" make Sloppy Joes? Is this really the only model of marriage assured of God's blessing?

My upbringing would suggest so. I was raised in a traditional Christian home with a fairly strict environment and conservative values. My family went to church every time the doors were open (or so it seemed). My father worked and my mom stayed home with me and my brothers and sisters. Her life revolved around all of us, meeting our every need at the sacrifice of her own. I don't even remember being aware of her needs. Like most children, my world revolved around me and my own immediate desires; the same was true for everyone else in our family. My dad came home, and dinner was soon on the table. Clean clothes were needed, and there was Mom—always with a pile of laundry, shirts, and handkerchiefs waiting to be ironed. Such was the routine. She never went out with friends. There were no girls' nights. I don't remember her having any hobbies of her own simply for enjoyment. Her children's needs and those of her husband were all that she ever looked to meet, and it wasn't even that her needs came last. They simply didn't come in any place at all.

What's more, she never seemed to disagree with my father. I've never heard her lament struggling with the kinds of pressures or conflicting messages that I struggle to sort out. I've never heard her say she had any regrets about how she chose to do things; indisputably, she raised successful children and in what seems a loving and faithful marriage to this day.

Can you argue with those results?

The thought hits me like a ton of bricks. If this is the picture of what it means to be a good wife, a submissive wife, then marriage *is* exceedingly hard work and not just in the clichéd "hard times" that everyone tells you will come. No, this kind of marriage is difficult every single day. To keep this kind of commitment with the excellence and honor that I want to give requires something that may be more than I've been in the mood to give or feel I'm even capable of giving.

What makes it so hard? After all, I was raised to be a caring and considerate person. I'm educated. I've plenty of common sense. I'm used to working hard. Doesn't anything really good require hard work, whether it's a promotion at work, running a marathon, climbing Mount Everest, or giving birth? Isn't even a vacation that much more enjoyable and appreciated after slaving the weeks beforehand?

For one thing, with any of those challenges, when you eventually reach your goal, like the top of your Mount Everest, you can revel in the beauty and exhilaration. But in marriage, the hard work never ends. There's no one lasting moment when all the world's problems are solved and you walk off into the sunset, barefoot on the beach, and the music plays and credits roll.

So does wanting that one lasting moment make me the most selfish person in the world?

Sometimes I think so. I truly think it's entirely possible that no one is more selfish—and I hate myself for it. So many women have lost their husbands to war or sickness, and I get annoyed by the "little" things that crop up, like when I can't go to bed when I want, or when I can't skip dinner when I don't feel like cooking, or when I have to go out and do something I'm not in the mood for. And you better believe that I don't want to have sex when I don't feel like it. I think, *Does my body belong to me now or doesn't it?* The Bible says once you're married, you become one with your husband and your body is not your own—so does that literally mean that my body can be touched by my husband any time, any place, whether I like it or not? That he can just grab my rear because he feels like it and I have to enjoy it? Or, if I'm exhausted from the kids, the day, the kids, my work, the kids . . . that I still have to feel sexy and sensuous just because he's in the mood?

Listen to how obnoxious I am, I think. I'm ashamed of myself, because my husband isn't a pig or some jerk. He's very caring about my needs. He isn't doing anything wrong. So am I? Is it so wrong to want to maintain possession and control

25

of my own body, personality, and likes, dislikes, and desires? Don't Christian parents drill into the heads of adolescent girls, "make him respect you"? But what does that even mean when it comes to the issue of "dying to yourself" in marriage?

What adds to my angst over these questions is that I hear the word *submission* tossed around far more than I think it deserves. Submission is only mentioned in the Bible a handful of times, yet it dominates sermons, conversations, and Bible studies as if salvation hinges on it. But does anyone else see the tension here and wonder if, in all honesty, we've overused and misunderstood the term *head of the household*? (I've tried not to ask this out loud in an effort to avoid public flogging.)

My husband has never used that term. What does it mean, anyway? That only one spouse has the decision-making power in a relationship? How can any spouse contribute as an equal partner to finances, or anything else in a marriage, if one opinion doesn't count as much as the other? Getting a trump card just because you're the guy doesn't seem true to God's design.

The thing is, I never hear Christian women discussing these things; sometimes I fear getting branded by a scarlet *F*—for feminist—for even raising these questions. And yet . . .

I see beleaguered wives in church, dragging their kids around and taking them out of the service when they act up while their husbands get to sit there and hear the rest of the sermon. I see the friend whose parents try to squash her nagging doubts about a marriage proposal because it may be her only chance to get married—or so they fear. I've been to the party for couples where the guys watch the game on TV while the wives prepare the food and watch the kids. *Why,* I wonder, *don't the wives get to watch the game?* Okay, so it doesn't have to be the game. There are three hundred other channels!

I don't want the marriage that I've seen too many times where the wife's needs are last, each and every single time. But I do want a godly marriage. I want to be the wife I should be. Just because other Christian wives do it a certain way doesn't necessarily make it right. I don't want to write off those voices that say to a wife, *Take time for yourself. Meet your own needs. Don't put yourself last all the time.* These things make some sense. How long can you dip down into an empty well, after all, and still find something to give? Didn't God create us with certain needs?

The institution of marriage asks a great deal of me, and I know it will continue to do so. All these questions I wrestle with in my marriage—the judgments, feelings, and doubts—have unearthed something spiritual, something about my relationship with God. Perhaps that's one of the intentions God had all along. Perhaps he wants these reflections on marriage to make us look more closely at ourselves and ask if we're not so much questioning submission to a husband as questioning submission to him. Maybe God's intention is to swiftly wipe out any illusions about ourselves and instead keep us honest, keep us real.

Marriage surely exposes the naked version of the self, all the selfishness or selflessness, all the stuff we're not so quick and eager to see. And yet, there it is.

Now what will I do with it?

2

Kate

growth in adversity

Wasn't marriage, like life, unstimulating and unprofitable and somewhat empty when too well ordered, and protected and guarded? Wasn't it finer, more splendid, more nourishing, when it was, like life itself, a mixture of the sordid and the magnificent; of mud and stars; of earth and flowers; of love and hate and laughter and tears and ugliness and beauty and hurt?

Edna Ferber

My marriage began with a magical romance and all the promise of the beginning of something wonderful. A fairy tale wedding ended with our departure in a horse-drawn carriage, my shoulder-length veil fluttering in the breeze and a sixpence in my shoe for luck as we waved good-bye to the people most dear to us in the world. All the dreams of my short lifetime culminated at the moment we rode off into the distance, into some bright unknown. We were young but responsible and prepared, as much as two people can be for the unknown . . . only . . . in a fairy tale, what's in the distance doesn't exist. At the end of a novel or a movie there's no future, no . . . *more*.

For us, though, the "happily ever after" of our wedding was just a beginning. We expected more to come. A script had been written . . . hadn't it?

For me the script began with my upbringing in a strict Christian household with very defined values, clear dos and don'ts. A big don't that I'd been taught all of my life—I'd been threatened, really, and bribed, and scared to death—was not to have sex before marriage.

Naturally, this was difficult. With every dating relationship there were temptations, and the unoriginal excuse that "everyone is doing it" was actually true. Everyone was doing it. Even though my friends were raised similarly to the way I was, they'd thrown off those encumbrances, whether premeditated or not, and tasted things I'd never dared to taste. They never pressured me exactly, but I always felt naive and on the outside of a grown-up club.

All the while I knew my time would come—and it would be the most wonderful because I'd waited. I even reasoned that my friends' and schoolmates' marriages were possibly doomed from the start because they'd gone ahead and had sex. So I felt bad for everyone doing it—really—but I was also self-righteously glad that I wasn't like them, that I'd waited, and that sex with my husband would be so worth the wait. God was going to bless my marriage, after all. I knew all this because every adult in my young life had told me so: parents, youth pastors, chapel speakers, Sunday school teachers—and I believed them, every one. I really did.

A few months before the wedding, however, I noticed it wasn't quite so difficult to wrench myself away from my fiancé and schlep home after a long good-night kiss. I wondered if all my hard-won willpower was finally becoming habitual—annoyingly ironic since in a short time I wouldn't be needing it. Yes, soon my trusty sexual willpower could take a long-needed vacation, I told myself, and it didn't need to come back, because when it went on vacation, I'd be on one too—with my new husband in Jamaica.

By the time I noticed this shift, this ebb of sexual desire, wedding preparations were constant and all consuming. *Maybe,* I thought, *all this busyness is what's distracting me.* Or maybe it was the knowledge that the grand moment was almost here, so it was much easier to bide my time. Regardless, I wasn't worried and never gave the change a second thought.

Then that glorious night arrived!

Only I didn't feel all that glorious. At the time I told myself it was nerves or fatigue. Our wedding day had been huge, long, and exciting, and I was spent. I'd wakened early and spent the morning in the hair salon with my wedding party; then with five hundred bobby pins sticking in my head it was off to the church to dress and begin the hours of pre-wedding pictures. I sat patiently under the talented hand of a hired makeup artist and listened to my dearest friends chattering and laughing. Then I began the long ritual of dressing, unwrapping my carefully chosen lingerie from the tissue paper, putting on my tulle-layered slip and arranging all the layers, being fitted and finished in my dress, and finally slipping into my shoes. Every detail had been planned and produced so painstakingly after hours of deliberation.

By the time the actual wedding started, I'd already had a full day of wedding pictures. My lower back was throbbing, and then my abdomen began to cramp. I tried to brush away both pains. This was my wedding day, for heaven's sake! I was supposed to be smiling all the time. How is it that even smiling began to hurt?

No matter, I told myself. *Nothing is going to ruin my wedding.*

Yet even now, years later, to recall that night is misery.

The hour-long ceremony went as planned, followed by a three-hour reception where we danced and toasted. We greeted guest after guest, all sweetly overwhelming me. I just couldn't believe all these people had come to see me get married; I was deeply touched by their presence.

When we finally got to our hotel that evening, late as it was, I hardly felt like ripping off my clothes and jumping into the sack. For one thing, I didn't want to take off my dress at all. I knew I'd never wear it again. So after delaying the inevitable as much as I could, I went into the bathroom to shower and change. Slowly I peeled off my wedding dress and put on my beautiful white satin nightgown that I'd so meticulously chosen. I then proceeded to attempt to mummify myself in the white, fluffy terry-cloth hotel bathrobe. Very sexy, right? I finally emerged from the bathroom, and I won't say any more about that night except this: we were two totally ignorant, complete novices. Was there really any hope for great sex that night?

31

The thing is, the sex never got better. We made disastrous attempt after attempt, but I never felt in the mood and absolutely dreaded bedtime.

We did keep trying—a few times every week. I never wanted to; I was so reluctant and uncomfortable that sex was entirely unenjoyable for me. I actually felt relief the nights when there was a likely chance my husband wouldn't try anything or didn't. And I wasn't that great of an actress; I'm sure he sensed my lack of enthusiasm. I know he felt rejected and utterly disappointed.

Before marriage, you hear all these stories about how often newlyweds do it—all the wild, passionate sex in unusual places. I don't know if those stories are true, but you think they will be for you. So here my husband was expecting sex at least every night, and instead it was at best two or three times a week—and it wasn't that good. Bitterness started between us.

I went to my gynecologist four or five months after the wedding for a checkup and told him the problems. He was very sympathetic and kind but said there didn't appear to be anything medically wrong. Ruling out a medical issue, I called around to find a therapist. Through a national Christian counseling center I found a woman with the letters "Ph.D." after her name. I thought this would ensure expertise and insight for my problem. I didn't think I could afford to waste any more time with anyone amateur, someone who wouldn't be able to "fix" the problem—and fix it quickly.

I was so nervous to meet this stranger and talk about something so personal, but during my first appointment I spilled my guts and I cried. I figured the only way to get anywhere was to be honest; such was the intensity of my grief that I absolutely couldn't talk about this without collapsing into tears.

The counselor mostly took notes and didn't say too much, and that seemed okay.

At my second appointment, exactly one week later, I sat down on the couch in her office and waited for the cue to begin. She just looked at me, so I awkwardly recapped and stumbled on about how everything was still the same as last week. It soon became very apparent that this counselor didn't remember any of what I'd wrenched from the depths of my soul last week. She even asked if she could take a moment to review her notes.

Aghast, I sat in awkward silence, thinking about what fraction of my hard-earned hundred dollars I was wasting while she did her homework. Worse than the monetary cost was the emotional toll. I felt foolish. Her inability to recall my situation made me feel like one of the masses. I knew my problems were just another case, just another job to her. But to me these problems were incredibly personal and traumatic. My whole world was turned upside-down. I was prepared to vomit it out any minute! As overly dramatic as it may sound, my whole life revolved around my husband's and my issues with sex, and things only seemed to be getting worse. Even then I think I knew the nightmare that was in store for us over the next few years, and I was starting to panic.

So after this counselor reviewed her notes and we talked a while longer, she offered this advice: "It takes some time to get things working well sexually with couples. It's only been four months. I think it should take at least take six. It will all work out."

It will all work out? It had already been seven months. I tried again to tell her that my husband's and my problems weren't just awkwardness or unmet needs. I had no desire. Nothing. *Nothing.*

She dismissed me and then mentioned something she'd heard on *Oprah.*

I wanted to scream. *I'm paying you one hundred dollars an hour, and you're telling me I can just sit home, watch TV, and get help for free?*

Instead, right then, right there, I made up some story about why I was unable to continue my counseling. Things were busy at work. Finances were tight. Blah blah blah. The counselor just nodded, and I left, humiliated. I'd shared uselessly, and I was lost. Where did I go for help now?

In the meantime, my husband and I continued our pattern in the bedroom, and we were miserable. I was a perfectionist, and both my feelings and my behavior were unacceptable to me. I felt like a complete and utter failure. Before marriage, I'd envisioned that to the outside world I could appear proper, even conservative, but at home I'd be this sensuous, sexy wife satisfying my husband's every need. I wanted to be like that country song about seeing the girl in a different light—the girl at the office whom everyone sees one way, but he knows differently. That was not how my marriage was playing out, and there wasn't a thing I knew to do about it. Never before had I experienced such complete helplessness.

Desperate, I decided to risk seeking advice from the wife of the pastor who had taken my husband and me through premarital counseling. This was even more difficult than that first appointment with the counselor. It had been one thing to share my most intimate issues with a professional who was legally bound to silence, but to someone I knew socially? This seemed entirely different, an incredible breach of privacy. Compounding my angst was the fact that I was used to projecting an image of having it all together—a reputation that just came about on its own, but that I tried to live up to. Plus, I'd been raised in a very reserved home where folks never aired the proverbial dirty laundry.

But I had no better ideas, and the Thelma-and-Louise-type exit I'd recently seen on the silver screen was starting to look not so bad.

I picked up the phone and called my pastor's wife.

We sat in my car on a warm autumn afternoon, and I spilled my long and gloomy story.

"That's just how it is for some people," she said. She added that she had the same problem in her marriage—she didn't really enjoy sex. "That's just how some people are," she repeated, maybe trying to convince herself as much as me. Her advice? Try to make the most out of other aspects of our marriage. She was kind and sympathetic, but that was it.

Briefly, after leaving her, I was placated. *So there isn't just something wrong with me. There are others with the same problem. I'm normal.*

Later, though, when the colors of the night became a romantic hue, I rebelled. *No, no, no! This cannot be just how it is. Why would everyone else say how wonderful sex is? If sex isn't really that important, why is it the source of demise for so many relationships?*

Worse, all the things I'd been told that sex would be if it was reserved for marriage seemed a lie—one enormous lie, a curse even. I'd obeyed all I'd been taught and not had sex before I married with the promise that God would honor my obedience. Instead, sex was the single source of heartache for my husband and me. This was not honor or blessing or a gift. I'd been looking for someone to blame, to lash out at; finally I found him.

You promised, I told God internally. *So now what is this?*

Still my husband and I tried. On our one-year anniversary we tried sex again, after a few months of making no attempt. Afterward, ironically, we heard fireworks outside. I turned my head away so my husband couldn't see the tears escaping my eyes. Though I tried to hold them back, the tears rolled down my face, soaking my pillow. I was so hopelessly sad.

I don't know, but maybe he saw my tears without my knowing, because that would be the last time we would try to have sex for four years. There was something unspoken, like we both knew this was how it was to be for a long time. Maybe forever.

I can't tell you how many nights I sobbed on the bathroom floor. I cried my body weight in tears on a regular basis. Sometimes I cried so hard I nearly vomited. I begged God for a miracle, a remedy, some solution. Again and again I begged for help.

I felt only silence in return. I can't say for sure, but I think I experienced the same feelings of a woman who can't get pregnant and desperately wants to—it's like you know in your heart that it's something so right, so natural, and everyone else has it, but you're shut out, an unwelcome intruder to the party.

That's when it seemed like sex was everywhere: in magazines, on television, in conversations with friends. If my husband and I saw a movie together and there was a romantic scene, I felt awkward. *For crying out loud,* I concluded, *sex is*

used to sell anything and everything—a story, an idea, a product.
When my friends lamented how strong their own sex drives
were, I felt even more crushed.

Here's the strange thing. When it was time for bed and the
lights were out, our hearts were like open, oozing sores, and
all we did was hurt each other. But the rest of the time our
relationship was okay. It really was. We enjoyed time with each
other. We talked about anything (but *that*), were silly together
and laughed, and took trips and spent most of our free time
together. We were friends, and I think we consciously held
on to that to survive.

So do I not love him? I wondered. I scrutinized my head and
heart, trying to get to the source of the problem on my own.
Would I be different with someone else? That was a dishearten-
ing thought to be sure, since if that were the case, I was now
stuck in a marriage that might never be good. I looked as deep
inside my soul as I could, scouring for an answer or even a
problem that I could solve to put all this behind me.

My bitterness grew. I was truly sorry I'd waited to have sex
until I was married. I told myself that if we hadn't waited, this
would never have happened. We would have either worked
out the kinks or decided we weren't sexually compatible and
then gone our separate ways. I began to think I was being
punished for doing the right thing.

Years went by. I walked on eggshells, it seemed. My husband probably did too. Most of the time he was able to be
emotionally strong, to give me the benefit of the doubt, trust
that I loved him, and make the best of things. But when he
was weak, as we all are at times, his hurt and frustration were
naturally aimed at me. He felt that I was paralyzed and doing

37

nothing. We said things to each other that we can never take back and never forget.

I truly didn't know what more to do. I'd tried everything. To add to my sense of helplessness, I read a book by a collection of Christian psychologists and sex therapists. One of the contributors mentioned in his credits that he was a professor at a Christian university. I went online to find his email address, contacted him, and briefly poured out my heart with a plea for help. I said I was at the end of my rope, had nowhere to turn, and was desperate. Did he know someone I could contact for counsel?

The professor's reply was short. "I'm sorry," he said. "I know no one in your city."

That was it. Later I discovered that one of the contributors to his book was actually from my city. I know it seems un-Christian, but I still wrestle with forgiving such a brush-off.

Meanwhile, my husband and I continued to work on every other aspect of our relationship. That was all we knew to do. *Maybe if we fix other things, the sex will eventually work out,* I thought. We rarely fought about anything else. We assured each other we were in this for the long haul and probed our personalities for every quirk to smoothen, every sharp angle to straighten. We confronted each other with honesty on our other issues too—perceived selfishness or thoughtlessness, compromising on how we spent our free time, allowance of personal space, and determining who would hold the checkbook and pay bills. We both tried to improve, to be better mates. At times we somehow put that one enormous problem of sex into a box so that we could be happy and enjoy our companionship with frivolity. But if ever the door to the dungeon was opened, the ugly monster inside would leave us retreating to lick our wounds for days.

I ended up seeing two more therapists for a short time. Both were good; I especially connected with one. While I didn't feel that I was making progress with my sexual issues, I worked on some spiritual and personal issues. I began questioning everything. What was peace? What was contentment? This therapist understood my questionings and worked with me as I looked for a more real understanding of all the biblical ideas and phrases that had become cliché to me: "Just trust in God" or "He works all things together for good" and "Delight thyself in him."

I wanted to yell out, "What on earth does all that mean?"

The foundation of my faith was rooted in the belief that Jesus died on the cross for my sins, but I began to realize my faith was also rooted in rewards. It was like I'd been operating spiritually on a quid pro quo basis—giving something for getting something, a sort of "I obey, now you bless me" rule. All my life I'd played by the rules, but my obedience wasn't out of a real love for God. I wanted my life to work and believed he would do that for me *if* I did certain things. And now I wasn't reaping the reward I expected.

I saw the same expectations in church, all around me: too many false formulas, too much lack of honesty, too many people operating on the false idea that if we're spiritual enough and, yes, good enough, God will cause things to go our way—and if they don't go our way, then we are doing something wrong. As a result, no one shared their struggles. I didn't either. *How hurtful*, I thought, *not to let others know when things are bad, all because of a fear they might think you unspiritual. How painful to live amid private muck much of the time.*

But these realizations were life changing for me. I was plumbing the depths of my soul and coming alive to new parts of myself—especially a true faith like I'd never known before. Somewhere in the process I no longer felt silence from God. I began to see the God whom I didn't really know, though I'd been a Christian almost my entire life. God wasn't purposely ignoring me; he wasn't distant when all I heard was silence. I'd just been looking for a character of his that wasn't real or right—God as Fixer or Rewards-Giver or Crutch.

God is so much more.

For a year this revelation became clearer and clearer, and my desire to know God became stronger. For me, this was an enormous step of faith, because there still wasn't an immediate solution to the problem my husband and I faced.

Instead, our problems went on a very long time.

Hanging on to our marriage for dear life, we were finally directed to a sex therapist by one of the previous counselors I'd seen. I wasn't too excited about seeing another therapist, one more man hearing the most intimate details of my sex life, or lack of one. But I pretty much had no choice. It was this or nothing—and my husband couldn't take nothing anymore.

So I sat in dire mortification for an hour every weekend. *No one belongs in your life like this except your spouse,* I thought, and I hated it. I had no hope—and I expressed that. The thought of living this way forever was unbearable. To this therapist's credit, we talked through many of the issues my husband and I had worked through between just us in a futile attempt to fix our problem, things like it was okay for me to say no to sex.

I'd been doing this, of course, for four years, but I was teeming with guilt about it. Now this therapist was encouraging: it's *not* wrong to refuse to force yourself to do something that's supposed to be so special, intimate, and for the enjoyment of both partners; you could actually psychologically damage yourself in association with sex . . .

Don't give up, the therapist encouraged. So my husband and I worked during the week, discussing and doing the homework assignments we'd been given. I regularly expressed my hopelessness. I didn't feel as if anything was changing. But our therapist was patient and persistent.

One Friday night after my husband and I spent a very enjoyable evening together—a concert and visit to a hip new restaurant—I settled into bed. I wasn't so averse to something physical happening between us, I realized. I'd never felt this way before, so I decided to move on the feeling, much to my husband's utter shock.

That Friday night became an entire week.

In all our married life we'd never had a week like that. We both sensed that to analyze this would be to jinx it, so we decided to just ride the wave as long as it lasted.

Later I realized I happened to be late taking my birth control pills. I'd forgotten to fill the prescription and had actually gone ten days without having the pill in my system. *Is it possible that the pill has been causing my aversion to sex?* Things were just too coincidental . . .

Before getting married, I'd read how some methods of birth control could diminish sex drive. A few months before my wedding, when I started on the pill, I'd talked to my doctor about this. I'd been nervous about gaining weight or becoming "hormonal," so my doctor had prescribed a "better, gentler" pill. I'd never noticed any side effects.

Now, though, I had questions, especially since once I began my scheduled doses of the pill, the wave of newfound ease

41

with sex crashed. My husband and I returned to our original patterns with disappointment and frustration.

The next time we saw our therapist, we told him all about it. He asked a lot of questions, concluding that the pill could be causing our problems. It seemed like I was reacting very strongly to the estrogen, he said. All the better pills, which it sounded like mine was, were high on estrogen, he noted. He asked if I'd be willing to stop taking them and see what happened.

I did so immediately.

The rest, as they say, is history. It seems crazy, all those years and thousands of dollars on therapy when both the problem and solution were so simple. In the end, I guess you could say my birth control pill really did its job.

Today my husband and I are light years from where we were one year ago. No, I haven't turned into a nymphomaniac. I still get tired and don't always feel in the mood. But I know that's normal. The important thing is that I no longer feel like I'm going to take a baseball bat to anyone who touches me.

When I recently—finally—told a friend about my husband's and my ordeal, she said she couldn't believe he stayed with me through it all. I know she's right. I also know it's sad that sex can play such a pivotal role even if two people really want to be together.

The truth is, my husband and I can't believe we made it either. It still hurts to look back over our first years of marriage. What we went through was too painful for us to say we're glad we went through it. But the experience has helped us realize how important friendship is in marriage. I see how we probably worked through some differences right away that would have taken years to work through otherwise. We have a stronger marriage, and I learned so much spiritually.

But was going through this extremely painful time the only way I could see how I reduced God to being my reward giver? Was this the only way I could have known the incredible commitment, patience, and love of the man I married?

I don't know. What I am sure of is that my marriage has been such immensely hard work. Though marriage is not my, or any woman's, entire identity, it's such a part of us that it reaches into the core of our being—and in order for it to truly succeed, we must allow it to do so.

My husband and I still have many years ahead, and I expect there will be more trials. There's something bittersweet about this. The bitter is, of course, obvious. The sweet is subtler. It is how coming through to the other side flavors my marriage. It is looking at my husband as I've never seen him before and feeling a greater appreciation for who he is and who I am; it is knowing we're battered and bruised, but we can stand up and brush ourselves off and say, "We made it."

With that, we can begin the next stage of life together.

3

Elizabeth

boundaries

Couples are wholes and not wholes, what agrees disagrees, the concordant is discordant. From all things one and from one all things.

Heraclitis

When Christian couples marry, they frequently light a traditional unity candle during the wedding ceremony. To start, the unity candle stands, unlit, between two single candles in a gilded candelabra. The single candles, already burning, represent each individual. At a key point in the wedding ceremony, the bride and groom step forward, take these burning candles on each end of the candelabra, and move as one to the unity candle.

Together they ignite the candle at the center.

Once the unity candle burns bright, both man and woman extinguish the flame on the single candles they each hold—the ones that represent their individual lives. Two thin lines of smoke rise into the air until, as the ceremony continues, even the wispy smoke vanishes. Light, once animated and alive on each of these single candles, is now erased.

Extinguished light, the darkness, seems gloomy to me: an end. Think about it: the conclusion of a merry candlelit dinner or the finishing of a warm and tranquil evening curled up by the fireplace. There's no warmth, no more magical glow and light.

What a contrast to the celebration that is a wedding—it's about beginnings, not endings.

So is it a beginning or an ending that causes most couples to blow out the candles that represent their individuality? Is their union meant to extinguish the existence of the two individuals? Does one surrender all? How much togetherness does a successful marriage require? Where are the boundaries in a healthy marriage?

I've been married for four years, and I still don't know the answer to that question. I grapple with it, both consciously and unconsciously, even after witnessing good role models.

I grew up in a very traditional Christian home. My mother stayed at home with me and my brothers and sisters, and my father was the breadwinner who provided for our family more than adequately. We were at church three times a week. We went to Christian schools all the way through university and graduate work. There was no question what our values were: hard work, resourcefulness, self-control, and respect for our parents. These virtues were so greatly esteemed in my family that everything we did seemed measured by them. My family was always very close, perhaps even a little enmeshed; family always came first—before friends or anyone else.

After going away to college, I tested the boundaries of those four walls of family for the first time. I was delighted by the wide-open space of freedom and embraced my independence and free will. I really began to develop who I was, to think for myself, to determine my own ideas about faith, politics, and how I conducted my life. I began to think independently about what I wanted my life to represent and what my future would look like.

Still, I got married young, just after completing college. I don't know whether I married because I still needed that feeling of family togetherness, or, on the contrary, because I wanted to gain my independence. Regardless, my family, like so many other Christian families, encouraged the marriage. My friends all married young too, and most before even finishing college. Why is that—the phenomenon that at so many Christian universities, students start developing a low-grade panic if they're beginning their senior year without a marriage prospect? Whatever the reason, I married a wonderful man. We are alike in many ways, yet we were raised rather differently. The fact that we were both raised in Christian homes is really the only commonality we share in that respect.

So we were married in the winter, and not too long afterwards, one glorious Saturday dawned sunny and temperate, the first warm day of spring that year. We decided to combine our weekend responsibilities with taking advantage of the mild weather and wash our cars—together. After piling my backseat with buckets, soap, brand-new giant sponges, and ratty rags, we each drove our vehicles to the car-washing pavilion of our apartment complex. This was a carport area with a vacuum and a couple of old hoses.

Side by side, we began to wash our cars. He washed his, and I, true to my nature, meticulously worked away on mine, careful not to miss a spot. Occasionally I'd break from my concentrated washing, and we'd teasingly spray each other or throw a wet sponge. That's what couples always do in the movies at least, so I felt like we should too, just to make sure we were having fun.

Still, I was taking the cleaning of my vehicle seriously, another value I had learned growing up. *Take care of your hard-earned possessions and never take them for granted.*

After a while, though not finished with his car, my kind husband strayed over to my area and started sponging my car, the part I hadn't gotten to yet.

I know it might seem silly, but this disturbed me. I looked at him with puzzlement and asked what he was doing.

He looked at me as though the answer to that question was pretty obvious. "Uh, we're washing our cars together," he ventured.

"No," I said, "you wash your car and I wash mine at the same time—that's together."

He laughed. "No," he said. "We're supposed to help each other—that's how we wash cars together."

Silently I fumed. I didn't need help, and I didn't want it. I had a certain way of washing my car, and he was mucking it up!

Now, I'm not a control freak. Really.

But this event did raise the question in my mind of what is "together"? We all know couples who fall into one of two categories. There's the weird togetherness, and then there's normal togetherness. Weird would be those couples who are joined at the hip, who seem to be so codependent that one person never does anything without the other. Men think the guy is "whipped," and women think the wife is simply pathetic. Truthfully, I've always looked down on these couples. I'm ashamed to admit it, but I especially look down on the woman because it seems she's sold out when she really needs to stand on her own two feet.

Then I wonder if my disdain for this kind of wife is rooted in jealousy. Maybe I wish I were more like her. Maybe I think the together-together couples have a marriage with a better chance of lasting.

On the other hand, I know many couples who have a degree of independence that works fine for them, maybe even better. They travel frequently and independently of one another, and the time they do spend together seems more quality because it's intentional and deliberate.

And then there are the couples who don't share the same interests or activities at all. They seem to bring something exciting and interesting to their relationship because they're developing themselves as individuals, not only as a couple.

The dilemma is, though, that I can think of couples who are examples of both kinds of togetherness, and none of their stories are complete—they still haven't made it through their entire lives together. The reality is that I really don't know what goes on in those relationships when no one else is around. Even if those couples do make it, who's to say it was because of "weird" togetherness or "normal" togetherness.

But I do look to other marriages around me and judge my theories, questions, and beliefs on what I see. I want my marriage to last, and I've been raised that barring any fundamental mess-up, like my husband being abusive, I've got one shot at this, so I had better do it right.

It's scary to think that even the seemingly little decisions could have long-term ramifications on the vitality and ultimate success of my relationship with my husband. What if I choose one way and it's wrong? I have two scenarios that play out in my mind. Behind Door No. 1, we've been married for forty years, and we have become too separate to make it work. We've become strangers, really, and in a last-ditch effort to save our floundering marriage we go to a counselor. I'm crying my eyes out in her expensive-looking office (no wonder it costs 120 bucks an hour), and she hands me the conveniently nearby box of tissues, looking sympathetic. My nose is now running, mascara gathered in dark pools below my eyes, and my husband, arms crossed, seems unmoved. He's indifferent to me now. So the counselor lowers her glasses, looks at me, and says, "You didn't surrender enough of yourself, you held on too tightly."

I sniff and protest, "But we did everything together, separately. What's so wrong with that?"

"You should have done everything together, together," she says, shaking her head.

I beg for another chance to do things differently, but now it's too little, too late.

But then there's Door No. 2. We've been married forty years, my husband starts avoiding being home, I think he may be having an affair (but then again, he has a big gut now and is no George Clooney), and I on the other hand still look pretty good. I've got good genes, and I'm aging gracefully. Still, in spite of my gorgeous good looks, I feel him slipping away and I become even needier (if that's possible). We stop talking because we're bickering all the time. I'm utterly lost without this closeness we've always shared. Finally, he leaves me, needing his space, not even willing to go for counseling, because he's having a midlife crisis.

As for me, I'm incapable of functioning on my own because my whole being, my whole identity is bound up in him. I've never done anything on my own, never even thought for myself. So then I stay home getting fat, eating potato chips on the couch, not working out anymore because we always did that together. I barely know how to get to the gym by myself. And he finds another woman to wash his car with, and now he has some flashy red convertible (because—remember?—he's in his midlife crisis).

See what I mean? Scary.

Who wouldn't want a formula that gives a guaranteed outcome—that answers what kind of togetherness to strive for? I get confused: do we wash our cars separately and yet together, still working together yet respecting individuality? Or do we go about this together-together, enmeshing everything in our lives?

In my more rational moments—and I do have those—I know there are more than two scenarios. Everything doesn't have to be worst case. But the reality is I'm scared of messing up. I love my husband and want so much to make our marriage work, but I also value my individuality. Before we married, I was just learning to be a little more independent than I was raised to be—and I liked that.

But what if there is a right and a wrong, if marriage does require only a together-togetherness to succeed?

What I fear is I am going to have to discover the right way for myself. I think that perhaps I'm afraid together-togetherness will encumber me and slow my steps. I fear that my newfound freedom will be lost and that my flight will be cut short only to compel me to return back within those four walls. And no one wants to live captive and restrained, at least not me, not when I've tasted of the eternal expanse of blue skies.

What I do know is this: healthy togetherness should never force me to give up who I am. Rather than lose myself, I should gain more of myself. It seems that marriage, if handled with care and mutual respect, has the ability to make me more myself than less. Rather than extinguish my one candle, I should use it to light another one, and then another and another. And perhaps it is the entire candelabra, with all the twists and curves, not only the center candle, that represents our union. The base of the candelabra, strong and rooted to the ground, gives way to expanse as it broadens its intricate arms holding many candles in a beautiful design. Like those candelabras you see at weddings that brilliantly twist and turn every which way. And the presence of many candles emanates a far greater light and glow than one candle ever could.

In his work *An Experiment in Criticism,* C. S. Lewis said, "The man who is contented to be only himself, and therefore less a self, is in prison. My own eyes are not enough for me. . . . Like the night sky in the Greek poem, I see with a myriad of eyes, but it is still I who see. Here as in worship, in love, in moral action, and in knowing, I transcend myself; and am never more myself than when I do."[2]

Well, Lewis wasn't necessarily speaking here of marriage, but his ideas apply. He has described exactly the togetherness I desire in marriage.

I see with a myriad of eyes . . . in love I transcend myself . . . I am never more myself . . . and it is still I who see.

4

Emma

confidence

A good marriage is one which allows for change and growth in the individuals and in the way they express their love.

Pearl Buck

I'm sixty-two years old, strong, and confident. I wasn't always this way. It's taken a lifetime of changing and evolving—and forty years of marriage.

To understand where I am, you have to know where I came from . . .

I was raised by my mother and father in an upper-class family. My mother and I had a mostly tumultuous relationship. I've often wondered why there's so much strife between mothers and daughters; it seems as if the relationship should be so innately pure and dear. Instead it's frequently the source of much disappointment all around. In any case, there are lifelong effects when a mother and daughter don't get along well. For me, this meant incredible shyness. My mother never said anything positive about me, so as a young child and then throughout my growing years, I was very timid.

My father, bless him, observed this for himself and always attempted to make up for my lack of instilled confidence. I have vivid memories of him telling me how talented and beautiful I was, how I could do anything. He wanted me to believe in myself. He constantly built me up.

In spite of this encouragement, I was never allowed to make decisions for myself. I was obedient and compliant, and my parents determined everything for me. As a result, I didn't really learn to think for myself and relied on others to make my decisions. I even became dependent on people for how I felt about myself and needed constant verbal affirmation—very shaky territory on which to stand.

It didn't help that I was of the sixties generation, raised by Pentecostals, and one of the very few of my women friends who went to college. The political feminist movement was getting started, and here I was, like all good Pentecostal girls of the time, planning to get married. Plus, I wanted to have sex—something good Pentecostal girls didn't do before marriage.

One of the first things that attracted me to my husband was the fact that he was college educated. Since I came from an educated and successful home, this was a big deal to me. The two of us together seemed rare in the cultural climate of rebellion and hippies. *We are the exception to the rule,* I thought. We dated for three and a half years before marrying.

When I got married, I was surrounded by myriad expectations, as most of us are, some reasonable and others not. So many events, both large and small, color and form your expectations, from the way you observe your parents to what your perceived needs are to what you've seen in movies or relationships that you really know very little about.

For me, many of these expectations were a result of the way my parents treated both each other and me. They were always very loving and respectful to each other, so that's what I expected for my marriage. But along with my expectations I brought a deep, crater-sized void of esteem and affirmation. My father had attempted to fill this vacant part of me, this constant need to be built up, but would my husband?

After our wedding, my husband and I adjusted to being together all the time, to developing a tolerance for each other, and, yes, to having sex (which, contrary to what I expected, was an adjustment too). As many women do, I sought to change the things about my husband that I wasn't comfortable with, until over time I learned that I can't change him. Rather, I must respect him the way he is. And I do—today I love and respect my husband for who he is. But that realization came over many years, and it required compromise—compromise a million times over on everything, from the littlest matters like his thriftiness versus my shoe fetish, to the life-changing decisions like where we would live.

So our marriage has been forty years of compromise.

The word *compromise* denotes concession and giving. But what's been so surprising to me is that even in the midst of compromise, rather than a person depleted of power, what emerged was strength. I surfaced stronger and more whole than ever before—not because I was half a person without a man before marriage, but because I gradually saw that to compromise my wants and ideas at times didn't mean I had to compromise who I was as a woman or a person. Yielding has never made me less important. My husband showed me that. He yielded to me just as much as I did to him, if not more.

He also showed me how we are equals. From the beginning of our marriage, he treated me as an equal in every way, except in physical strength, and in that respect he was always happy to help out when needed.

He also pushed me and persuaded me to be more intimate than I'd ever been. Self-conscious as I was, I always stayed on the surface with most people. I wanted to create an impression about myself that I could control. I was sure that if others were to know the real me, the person who resided deep within, they, like my mother, would have no words of compassion for me. So I always measured carefully everything I said and did. My husband would settle for none of that. He didn't need to hear about every mundane detail of my day, like what I had for lunch and other silly things I could have prattled on about. In our early years of marriage, these were the only things I verbalized to him, actually thinking that I was opening up myself. But he would push for more. He wanted to know what I thought and felt. He even wanted me to voice my disagreement with him if I felt it.

He forced me to make decisions for myself, not because he didn't care what I did but because he wanted me to see that I could think for myself; I was strong and capable. He valued my thoughts and ideas and wanted me to see their value as well. He was about empowering me, not crushing or competing with me.

As I've observed other relationships I've concluded that often Christians—men and women—seem to behave as though women are less important individuals. It's expected that our happiness is secondary to anyone else's, less important than the happiness of our spouse and children. I'm not sure who puts that on us as women. Perhaps we may do that to ourselves, a kind of martyr complex that makes us feel valuable.

But you know what? When you're my age, you never spend much time worrying about what other people's expectations are for you as a wife. All I care about are my husband's expectations, and I've always known what those were.

So we've built a life together, these four decades, and in that life I got a friend and a mate. I have intimacy, and my husband completes the person I am. Sex—what once was a rousing motivator for marriage—though still enjoyable, now no longer seems so important. I got so much more than permissible sex from marriage. I got something I never imagined or even asked for: I emerged as a more complete person. My work and sacrifice didn't just fall into a deep, meaningless abyss. Rather, I received the greatest and most significant gift from this man to whom I committed my life. I found a strength that I never thought possible and a self-confidence that I never thought I could attain.

I cannot imagine who I would have been had I married someone else. With all my expectations for marriage, developing a greater confidence and self-awareness was never one of those expectations.

I actually like who I became as a result of my husband, and I like who we became together. He always saw in me the possibility of achievement. He's never failed to tell me how intelligent and insightful I am. He builds me up, recognizing my talents and the unique things that I contribute not only to his life but to this world—the talents and gifts that were just part of me but that I'd always taken for granted and never saw as special. Somehow, he made them so. I never felt held back or that I was sacrificing myself or my potential by getting married, even though I was a bride at only twenty-two years of age.

Today when my husband tells me how proud he is of me, I realize his support has been the single most important contribution to my life. I'm no longer the shy little girl I once was. I'm transformed: self-confident, independent, but not superior, just a woman comfortable with people in all walks of life, a woman not easily intimidated. This transformation didn't happen overnight. It's a change that's taken a lifetime of loving, giving, receiving, and—yes—compromising.

Who would have thought that by compromising and giving up some things—no, many things—I would actually become more, not less? It defies logic, and yet there it is.

5

Rebecca

growing up

Marriage is our last, best chance to grow up.

Joseph Barth

If grown-ups are those who are confident, self-assured, living their purpose in life, and are able to pay the bills, take care of themselves, and forge new paths and traditions or ways of thinking and living, then I would say I married as a child.

It was marriage that made me a grown-up.

But what is a grown-up, really—and do you have to be one to have a successful marriage?

Lately I've wondered about this because I've realized how being an adult is like following the proverbial dangling carrot or its shadow. As you get closer to it, the impressions change, you see new angles; the destination constantly evolves, progresses, and matures.

I was raised in a loving and very close Christian home. We were taught that God should be a priority in our lives. With that we learned that appearances are of vital importance—the justification or motivator in everything we do. As a result I grew up afraid to be unique and insecure about who I was and what people thought of me. I learned a great deal about God, but I didn't really come to know who God is in a personal way until later in my twenties.

Though our home was conventional in most senses, there wasn't the customary balance of power. My father was the disciplinarian, and my mother was more sympathetic to our shortcomings and disobedience, far more laissez-faire. So my parents weren't unified in the way they wanted to raise their children, and I took advantage of this by working them against each other, obtaining permission and approval for something from one after the other had denied it, crying to my mom when I had been disciplined by my dad, or testing the waters more when my dad was traveling for business.

The issue was that my parents came from extremely diverse backgrounds and have spent their entire marriage trying to close that distance. It's like they're trying to reach some summit of common ground that I'm not sure will ever exist for them; watching them reminds me of the childhood game of chasing your shadow. There's all the futility, only without the merriment and laughter that game evokes.

However, the fact that my parents still strive to resolve their differences has shown me their commitment to family and to marriage, and that virtue I hold dear. In fact, it may be part of why I always wanted to share a life with someone, a husband, a family. I can't remember a time when I didn't. I was raised to desire that almost as a place of nirvana; taught there's nothing greater in life. So I always single-mindedly pursued that goal of creating a family. I only attended college because all my friends did, but I never graduated. I was never career oriented and never desired to work out of the home. Every aspect of marriage was always desirous to me.

Although my overdeveloped desire to marry was palpable, I didn't marry my husband out of mere desperation. I really believe God chose us for each other—I was created for him, and him alone. Even now there's no desire within me to be with anyone else.

My expectations of marriage, however, were based on an odd concoction of things, both things I liked or accepted and things I loathed or never understood. I'd sorted through these things, though not altogether intentionally, for what I wanted to keep and what I wanted to change.

My husband had done the same and brought along his own expectations based on his upbringing. The ironic twist is that his expectations were so very different from my own. So our union was as my parents' had been: uneven, with an imbalance of power, and full of chasing shadows. Why is it that so often the thing that seems to drive us craziest is the thing we somehow gravitate toward in the end?

We didn't have premarital counseling, because in our own way we'd talked and worked through many issues already. We rehashed our previous dating experiences and the mistakes we made, most before we even knew each other. With regard to sexual past, he was far more experienced than I was, and as I dealt with jealousy and insecurity, he assured me that our experiences together would be different. We talked of our individual teenage rebellion and our paths to faith.

We talked about many things except our expectations and how to blend our entirely different backgrounds and ideals.

Call this the highly dangerous combination of youthful arrogance and naiveté.

In hindsight, we spent too much time working on the past and not enough on the future. We both wanted a traditional home where he would be the main provider and I'd keep the house and stay home with our children when they eventually came along. But that was where our expectations came together like a marching band configuration and then peeled off, going separate ways.

His way included expectations like this: he would make all decisions exclusive of me (this would be his responsibility as "the Man"), while I kept house as his mother had. My way included the expectation that I was marrying into a partnership in which my opinion would be sought, valued, and heard, while he took care of "fatherly duties" (as my father had) like taking out the trash, locking up the house at night, and servicing our cars when they needed it. Who takes the car for an oil change seems like an insignificant, even silly thing, but no expectation is too small in a marriage. Even the simplest differences can fester and become a point of great contention.

So in the early years of our marriage, these unmet expectations were my greatest grief. I didn't feel valued as a person, or respected, or even necessary. Not only did my husband not seem to care about my opinion, but I didn't even know how to begin running a household as he expected. My mother had focused on quality time and relationships and never felt one person could do both this and keep a perfect house, so she didn't—she never really worked to keep her house. Though my dad always pitched in to help, my husband wasn't going to do that.

Add to all of this the birth of our son, and you can see how I was way out of my league. I was suddenly not just "the Wife" but "the Mother" in a marriage in which my value seemed to lessen, as did my identity as an individual. I was crushed; I didn't see things changing. Hadn't every wise person always said never to marry someone you want to change? People are who they are, right?

It seemed so. My husband was oblivious. Our roles were as he experienced growing up and believed they should be. So I remained silent. With friends and family, I was protective of my husband, even in my unhappiness, because I knew, though meaning well, they would only see my side. I couldn't depend on them for objective advice or opinions.

Things got worse. Desperate to please and a perfectionist to the core, I struggled and faltered under the weight of being a wife. The role seemed a burden, even when I earnestly tried to find my purpose and personhood in it. I was afraid to voice my feelings to my husband. I wasn't sure how he'd take what I was trying to say.

And all the while I had to keep taking out the trash myself.

Finally, with the birth of our second child and feeling as though there was no other choice, I fixed all my hopes on God. I prayed for him to change my husband and help us find some common ground.

God was waiting for me all along.

As I began to voice my feelings to my husband *and* to God, a funny thing happened. We labored on as two children still immature in our relationship, a little girl and boy yet parents of a little boy and girl, feeling the steady and sometimes sharp throb of growing pains while learning to be parents and spouses—and adults. We discussed things and groped for the right words with one another as though trying to step forward without losing our footing entirely. More difficult discussions ensued until slowly, slowly we grew and stretched and triumphed.

Rather, God triumphed. And his greatest triumph, something I never saw my parents share, is the common ground on which we stand.

By triumph I mean this: through my husband's growth came my own. That's one of the most painful and yet most beautiful elements in marriage, the way everything you do impacts the other person. Through watching him grow, I saw my own lack of trust in him and my insecurity. I began to melt from my frozen state of perceived inadequacy and attack my role with gusto. Somehow, seeing him change has shown me myself, and I feel confident. Now I feel like a woman rather than a girl. And I wonder and marvel at the way God answered my prayer and met the need of his child.

Today I finally have the partnership in marriage I so desired as a young girl. It's hard won, but my husband now values my input and wants my opinion. We still have a submissive marriage, one that many view as passé, but I'm confident and safe in that. I've come to a place where I'm secure as a person and a woman. I see my uniqueness. I know that I work hard and I'm successful in the management of our household, and I know my uniqueness is important to my husband and our children. I see myself as the backbone of our life together, and that's my purpose, so I embrace it and am content.

As with much of growing up, in some ways the growth has been bittersweet. With every bit of new ground that's gained, something's left behind: sometimes security, sometimes innocence, sometimes acceptance and approval. I guess that's why we look back on our childhood with nostalgia. We still want those things that are lost, and we still long for the time when it's okay to want them. No matter how grown up we become, we always want approval, especially from our parents. At my age now, I'm convinced that part of us almost always remains a child.

In my case I don't feel support from my family and my friends for the traditional path my husband and I have chosen. They don't understand our choices or how our relationship functions. So that's hard. I feel judged and not so safe with others and wish for community and a place of shared struggles and desires. I see the importance of openness, but even more strongly I feel the support of my husband—a support more intense than I ever could have imagined. That's part of growing up too: being content with the choices made and being strong enough to withstand the criticism that may come because of them.

We don't have to be like everyone else, and ultimately it doesn't matter what other people think, even the people we love. Given that I was raised to care so much about the opinions of others, that's been an enormous hurdle for me to choose not to jump over. But I'm doing it.

Now, in the same way you measure the growth of a child against a wall or door frame, I see the marks of growth in our marriage so far. I know we haven't yet reached our full height. There are more marks to be made. My husband and I will always be growing both together and separately; from time to time we'll again feel the pain of that growth. And what we deem as growth will continue to change and evolve. That's part of being grown-up too: knowing that in many ways you're still a child and that perhaps the place of being a true grown-up is a place you may never achieve no matter how old you get.

For now I'm safe and secure both in my husband and in the power and protection of God, and I like that.

Knowing that there is still much I haven't learned yet resting in the peace that comes with security and care, in that way, I hope I'll always have a little bit of childlikeness.

6

Jen

becoming one, dying to self

A good marriage is that in which each appoints the other guardian of his solitude. Once the realization is accepted that even between the closest human beings infinite distances continue to exist, a wonderful living side by side can grow up, if they succeed in loving the distance between them which makes it possible for each to see the other whole against a wide sky.

Maria Rainer Rilke

If I lived in a fairy tale it would go like this. There once was a girl who fell in love. She loved at first with abandon. She loved with grace and without judgment. She loved fully and completely, at least as much as a young girl can. Then one day the girl got married, and then another day sometime later she said, "When have I given enough?"

That's the defining question for me, the question that leads to a litany of others: is there a limit to giving in marriage? Do you give of yourself without end or do you keep a little of yourself for yourself? How much do you allow yourself to change to accommodate the other?

In real life I've been married for eight years. I was raised in a home where my mother gave herself to us and to my father entirely. She sacrificed everything for all of us and never met her own needs. I believe she found her worth and value in that.

She seldom shopped for herself, and when she did it was only for necessities. She cooked dinner every day. She woke up early to make our breakfast and lunches. She threw huge birthday parties for each of us every year, spending hours decorating a cake, sometimes even two cakes—one for a school party and one for a celebration at home.

I don't know that she ever sought her own interests, desires, or talents. It seemed her talent and purpose was being a mother—and she was very good at it. At least that's the talent she gave herself to . . . though now, through the eyes of an adult, I see that she had many, many gifts that she gave up.

Without doubt, I've been one of the primary recipients of her sacrificial giving, and yet I don't want that sacrificial role for myself. I see unquestionable benefits to the beneficiary, but the role of selfless benefactor isn't something I ever wish for. So, for right or wrong, my mother's example isn't something I've ever desired to fully emulate.

I can't say when or why I decided that.

I know it was before I got married, but I never gave much thought as to what that would mean until I had a home and husband of my own.

I never want to be characterized as a wife or a mother but rather as a person and as a woman who also happens to be a wife and mother. But sometimes I question this desire, especially when there's conflict. I wonder if the conflict exists because I made that choice. I wonder if I've brought the conflict on myself because I didn't do what my parents modeled. Perhaps I question my own way because that's not the example I was raised with or because that's not the example I see in many marriages.

In the eight years I've been married, my husband and I have had many differences in how we like to spend our time and what our personal needs are. At the core our values are in alignment, but it's in the everyday, even insignificant things that we are often worlds apart. And greater than that, our personalities are so very different; at times I feel like we take the whole Mars and Venus cliché to a new level. Does every couple feel like that at one time or another? Sometimes the differences seem entirely too great, even insurmountable. Then, especially in the midst of a fight that started out as a silly disagreement, I look at that man and wonder how we ever dated. Of course, I still love him, and deeply, but for a minute I can't think of one thing we have in common, and it mystifies me how we got as far as marriage in the first place.

It's not that I can't think of why I married him. That's not what I'm saying. It's just that I can't see how we found enough activities to do together or enough common interests to talk about that our relationship ever progressed.

But I guess I do know how that happened, and you probably do too because we've all done it—played that game couples play when they're dating. You know the one. You're so in love that you adore everything the other person does. You agree on nearly everything. You love all the same movies and songs. ("That's your favorite band? Mine too!" "You love cold pizza for breakfast? Me too!" "You love Italian food, and traveling, and hockey, and reading, and my favorite restaurant, and jogging, and long walks on the beach, and—it gets dreamier and dreamier, doesn't it?—dancing in the rain? Me too!") And it's not so much that you were lying. You really weren't. But after the initial honeymoon phase, things begin to sound more like this: "I said I like that? Well, Italian food is too fattening, and hockey is boring, and jogging hurts my knees, and the rain makes me catch cold . . ." In those early stages of romance and infatuation, you really do like any activity as long as you get to be with that person.

Am I right?

Eventually, we all go back to being who we always were.

At least that's how it worked for my husband and me, only now we're at a moment of truth, a crossroad . . . or maybe it's more like a roundabout. By that, I should tell you that we've fought for eight years about the same issue—our differences and how to compromise them so that life together is livable for both of us. Round and round we go, time and time again, allowing for short breaks of respite along the way. We call a truce for a while, and then our differences get to be too much for one of us, and we hop back on the merry-go-round again. Ah, rides that just go round and round always did make me sick.

We both know the script by heart. There have been hurt feelings and new resolves to compromise, and always with the best of intentions. Yet we're still so far apart on so many things. Now it seems that the only way to overcome the problem is for one of us to change . . . and so I go back to my original question: how much change is too much? When does it mean I'm compromising myself in a way that's wrong? When am I compromising for the good of the relationship, and when am I being untrue to myself and to whom God made me to be? When do I play the That's-Just-Who-I-Am card, and when am I compelled to make changes? Surely either option can be necessary at times, can't they? Have I sold my soul and my will to marriage? Sold my soul to this man I truly love but sometimes just can't find compatibility with? Do I have no ground to claim rights or to say, "Here I am, take it or leave it"?

When I was dating, my parents and all the voices of wisdom in my life said that no one should ever date and marry someone they want to change.

Who hasn't heard that before, right?

You either like the person the way they are or you don't.

Okay, so people supposedly don't change, but do the rules change when the stakes change? When it's marriage, when you're committed to love for better or for worse forever, do the rules of acceptance, sacrifice, and compromise change?

I'm beginning to think they do. They have to—that's what makes marriage. So maybe the inevitable question isn't "if" but "how much?"

In Philippians 2:7, it's written:

> But [he] made himself nothing,
> taking the very nature of a servant,
> being made in human likeness.

So Jesus made himself nothing. He emptied himself out, gave up who he was and all that he deserved. Jesus, the Son of God, dwelling in heaven with God, emptied himself to be a simple carpenter, to come to our imperfect world and be subjected to all it entails.

If I believe, then, that Jesus is the example for me, am I supposed to change who and what I am in order to "save" harmony with my husband—in order to love him in a way that gives glory and honor to God? And should my husband do this for me? And can I really change my character without looking back?

I'm sure that Jesus, who made the ultimate sacrifice, didn't resent God, or even feel bitter toward Adam and Eve for getting this whole sin thing rolling, for having to give up his position in heaven for a time and suffer for us. But I know I can't possibly be so selfless. I'm perfectly capable of sitting around and sulking over not getting my way, or even worse, manipulating my husband with a relentless martyr complex. Is selfish me capable of selfless sacrifice without keeping score?

I don't know all the answers to the questions I've raised. I know that if I sought advice from others, I could always find someone who will tell me what I want to hear. And that's what can be so frustrating. But I know there is no fairy godmother coming into this story to transform me into a new and improved partner or to instantly rescue us from our diversity.

I also know that my husband fell in love with me and me with him for a reason. We're still in love, despite our canyon—make that Grand Canyon—full of differences. Even with all the "me too's" of our courtship, I still saw the man I wanted to spend the rest of my life with, and he saw me for who I was too.

I have a fuzzy memory from kindergarten of learning about the essence and volume of water. It can change shape but still be the same. The same amount of water can be poured into a bathtub, expensive crystal stemware, or a swimming pool, but its volume and essence remains the same. In the same lesson we learned that five nickels or one quarter can still be twenty-five cents. It looks different, but it's still the same amount of money. So I can adapt my life to his, but I don't have to lose myself, my essence. Put another way, I can have costume change after costume change, but I'm still the same character, still the person he married. I don't want that person to go away, and neither does he. I really don't think I should change the person I am. In any case, I don't think I could. And yet . . .

There are a great many occasions when compromise is in order. That doesn't seem to change, no matter how seasoned a marriage is. There's a vital element to these compromises, sacrifices, or essence alterations. It's up to both of us to protect the other from giving up too much to the point that we are being taken advantage of, or to protect us from emptying ourselves to the point that our self-respect is at risk or we become arid and dry.

Maybe, if we can succeed in protecting the other, we can be uninhibited in the emptying of ourselves and know that we will not be depleting who we really are.

Maybe, then, the lesson is that Jesus emptied himself because he trusted the Father. He knew the whole story and trusted the outcome. Maybe I can give of myself with abandon because I trust my husband not to empty me dry. And he can trust me too. Maybe because he knows who I really am, he'll make sure I don't give that up to compromise.

The thing I believe, the thing I know, is that the outcome is worth it, and the ending priceless.

7

Amelia

the trinity
of marriage

The chain of wedlock is so heavy that it takes two to carry
it—and sometimes three.

Alexander Dumas

A few months ago I was at a wedding where the preacher,
who was sincere though at times platitude filled, spoke of
the fact that this marriage was not between two people but
three. He said that since the man and woman before him were
both committed Christians, God was to be the third person
in their marriage.

I've heard this at almost every Christian wedding I've ever
been to, but it especially struck me this time. *What does this
mean?* I wondered. *What does a marriage of three look like in actu-
ality, not merely theory? How can a being not living and breathing
in the flesh truly be a third person in marriage?*

I'm ashamed to ask this question, because it seems as if I should know the answer already. I was raised in a Christian home and attended all twelve years of Christian school and then four years at a Christian college. But if I were to be honest, even though both my husband and I are Christians, I don't feel as if God is the third person in our marriage. We go through the motions. I pray. He prays. We pray together before bed. We have nightly devotions. He reads from the Bible or a book of readings, while I often fight off the desire to let my mind go in a million different directions—and I lose that battle frequently. We attend church and Sunday school together. We're in a small group with other committed couples from our church. But these things all seem like things that we *do*, not who we *are*. Too much of our Christian walk is about things we do; what about how we should *be*?

I'm trying to answer these questions, not just in my head but in a way that I can truly live out. To begin, then, I've taken a raw look at my marriage.

My husband and I have been married three years. I was raised in a strict Christian home. My parents had both come from difficult and broken backgrounds but had developed a strong marriage. They had a mutual respect for one another, they rarely argued, and they seemed genuinely in love after many years of marriage. My father always looked out for my mother's needs, and she loved to do things for him. Cooking was not her duty, it was something she enjoyed doing for my father. They hated to be apart from the other. Their relationship always seemed perfect, and that was the marriage model for me. It was a good one.

Yet now as I look back through the veil of my own marital challenges, growths, and sometimes disappointments, I wish my parents had talked more about their mistakes and had open discussions about marriage and its realities. As a result of this lack of forthrightness, I entered marriage very naively, expecting much more of my husband than he could ever give. Even so, I married him because I loved him; there was a completeness I felt with him, something about him that I felt I couldn't live without.

Last year we went through a tough time in our marriage. We are both unbelievably inept at conflict resolution. We fight mean, and we were tearing each other down. We knew it too, so all the while I really did try to work through my differences and insecurities with him in a healthier, more loving way. I prayed earnestly but didn't really feel anything. I wanted answers to my prayers, but there didn't seem to be any forthcoming. There was no peace, no message, no miracle.

When I look at this, I see the irony: we often do have three people in our marriage. The third person just isn't always God. It's often my ex-boyfriend, or his ex-girlfriend, or his mom, or my mom . . . and I'm certain such will be the case when we decide to have a child. Obviously, these people aren't truly in our marriage, but they affect either my way or his way of thinking and feeling to such a great degree that it's almost like a literal third person is with us. It's like the children's nursery rhyme about too many bears in the bed: "three bears in the bed and the little one said, 'I'm crowded, roll over.'" Or to bring it back to grown-up terms, a metaphorical marriage bed can get rather crowded.

These people can seem just as real in the room as my husband and me, whether it's because of my innate need to please my parents, or our desire to bring the way we were raised into solving a conflict, or the way we carry past hurt or baggage from a previous relationship or jealousy over a former inti-macy, but we don't want them in our marriage. This presence is as irritating as the itch from a tag in a new sweater or as heavy as those extra five pounds gained last Christmas that you still can't shed—a constant reminder. And maybe that's just it. Maybe God, though he wants to be the third person in our marriage, doesn't want to be the third wheel—unin-vited, unwelcome except on the fringes. Maybe he wants us to consciously let him in.

I think about when we seemed at an impasse in our mar-riage. When we had no idea how to cross it and we felt so alone. I knew God couldn't have abandoned us, so it had to be something in me. Was God silent, or was I just looking for an easy answer that would make it all better, like what my parents would give me? Maybe, rather than work, I wanted to be bailed out, like the kid who waits until the night before to work on his science project only to take second place at the science fair, thanks to Mom and Dad, who remain thank-less. Maybe that's why I let into our marriage people who shouldn't be there—it's all too easy, and I'm looking for an easy answer.

I suppose I allow those other people—the unwanted bears in the bed—to control my thoughts, feelings, perceptions, and memories. But why is it so easy to let others (or even ourselves, so we think) control our lives; and why is it so hard to let God?

That's the key, the million-dollar question, for practically everything in my faith. I don't let God control my own life, so how can he be present in my marriage when I'm 50 percent of that union? It's through this dilemma in my marriage that I see a window into my heart.

76

I begin to see how I live a life of recipes and methods. The small group, the Bible reading, praying, and tithing—much of that is for the purpose of following a formula so that my life will turn out the way I want. I realize I'm doing the right things, but I'm using them to control the outcome of my life. If I follow the recipe perfectly, I'll end up with a gourmet dinner, a feast, rather than last night's leftovers or, worse, a burned meal that even the dog won't touch, right?

It's an absurd notion that I could contain God in a method, but that's what I've been doing. I wonder if God shakes his head at me ruefully and thinks, *Sometimes you just don't get it.*

So this is my challenge: relinquish control. And it scares me. It means if I walk out from under the canopy of formulas, I walk out knowing anything can happen. Of course, anything always could, but until now I've lived under blissful delusion.

So here's where that leaves me: I must approach God as I am. I must ask him to purge my current way of thinking and being. That means my husband and I need to spend time with God separately and then together as a couple. The state of our individual personal relationships with God will surely be revealed in our relationship together.

My dilemma is making this head knowledge real in the practical workings of my life. I must also learn to *be*, not only *do*. I don't know that this will ever stop being a challenge. I don't know that it will ever be easy for me or that I will ever get it completely right. But I know that I have to work and to try—and I know God will somehow meet me where I am every single time.

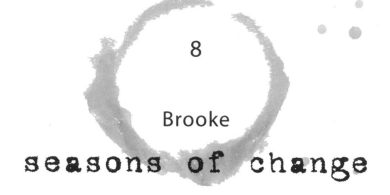

8

Brooke

seasons of change

A successful marriage is an edifice that must be rebuilt every day.

André Maurois

I've always loved season changes. Though I love some seasons more than others, the changes themselves are what excite me—the start of something new, the way it makes one aware of the passage of time.

Without transition, wouldn't life be less interesting, more flat?

I've been thinking lately of how much the life span of marriage is made up of seasons. The years seem to pass in phases and not necessarily year by year; some seasons can be two years long while others are six months.

There are winters, cold, gray, and frozen, where one spouse or sometimes both watch their branches stripped bare or frozen solid; all the attributes that exist in warmer weather—passion, warmth, openness, and joy—seem to have vanished. There are summers, hot, even steamy (why, though, do they seem the shortest season?). There are springs, times of discovery and growth in an individual or in the relationship, with everything suddenly new and vibrant; it's as if you're seeing your spouse for the first time. And then there are autumns, full of vibrant color and change, sometimes with chilly nights but also true blue skies and pure golden sunsets that assuage the coolness.

But what was it Robert Frost wrote? "Nothing gold can stay . . ."

I was raised in a fairly large family by Christian parents who are still married to each other. I didn't necessarily like everything I saw in their marriage, but they stayed together, and that was one expectation I had for myself. My marriage was going to last.

I always knew I wanted to be married and have a family, but I was never in any rush. I was very certain about what kind of man I was looking for, and I waited until I found him. I saw the world, chased all my dreams, and accomplished what I wanted. As a result, I got married later than many other women, and so my husband and I decided to begin having children right away.

By this time I was ready to settle down and stay in one place. I'd had my share of travel and that kind of adventure. I was more than ready for a different adventure altogether. Besides, I always wanted to be a housewife. I know that sounds politically incorrect, but it's true. I've done everything I wanted to before marriage, I told myself. Now is my season to settle in.

As I look over the seasons of our twenty-one years together, I see how my husband and I have been enriched by them. And I'm still growing immensely as a person, through the good times but mostly through the challenges and conflict. As we've had struggles with one of our children, grieved the loss of loved ones, experienced the challenge of relocating to a new city, and as I've watched the man I share my life with physically age, I have grown in my faith, in my ability to trust God and trust my husband, in my perspective of life and of myself. I've grown from a simple faith to one that is deeper and complex, I have a greater appreciation for the blessings that I have been given, and I have a greater understanding for the things in my life I would not have chosen but have been given.

Together my husband and I have seen many season changes, yet sometimes they still surprise me, sneaking up like an Indian summer day or a surprise cold snap in April. Often a long spring has lulled me into thinking, *We've finally made it; we've finally worked out all the kinks taming this thing called marriage; finally it's purring in our hands.* Then, like a roaring March lion, it's a beast again. I'm not sure if the transformation was made worse by the fact that I'd gotten comfortable and was savoring the sweet taste of victory. But isn't that how life is?

Spiritually, do we ever have permanent victory? Maybe in some things, but often what we've been able to make progress on by the grace of God will always be a bit of a thorn in the flesh. Meaning that there are some things we will always be tempted to do or think, even though we wish we wouldn't. We are who we are, to some degree. Our personalities, the way we see the world, the way our feelings and minds work. Isn't it like being born with brown eyes or blue? Neither one is better than the other—it is what it is.

This discovery was one of the greatest triumphs for me in my marriage: knowing that my spouse is the way he is because that's just who he is and not because he doesn't care or is trying to hurt my feelings or just really, really wants to tick me off. Our differences can be so beautiful, and yet in the dreariness of the deepest winters, at least one of us has found them insurmountable and has sometimes wondered why and how we ever got together. The blessing has been that we never both thought that at the same time.

Through all the seasons of our marriage, it seems there's been one constant, almost like our Achilles' heel, the one source of conflict that's demanded the most work, the one issue that just won't go away. Why is it that even the littlest of fights seems to come back around to that issue? As soon as we start fighting, I know exactly where we're headed and even how the conversation is going to go, but each and every time we fight it out and then retreat and try to make changes. And we do make some small changes, but the color of our eyes, the true source of the stalemate, always stays the same.

There has only ever been one time when I thought about giving up. One particularly dark and long winter I'd had enough and didn't want to do it anymore. I was sick of all the work. No one ever said marriage was going to be so much work—and it was relentless. Sometimes I thought that surely every marriage doesn't take this much work; it must be just ours. I was so tired, and I wanted out. I didn't care that it was wrong or who it would hurt. I was finished. I said as much out loud, and I think I really scared my husband.

81

In all the years since I had been a Christian, I had believed I could be honest with God in prayer. I'd been brutally honest with him many times. He can take it. If you read the Psalms, the psalmist expresses every emotion to God, and they are abundantly loud and clear. There's hope, sadness, anger, despair, questioning, and even accusation—sometimes all in the same psalm. So I went before God and I told him, in truth, that I was done. Then I asked him—no, begged him—for help with my unbelief: the unbelief in my husband, in myself, and in the vows I took.

That prayer sort of renewed my will, and somehow the two of us worked on our marriage again. And we got through that storm. God softened my heart—actually, both of our hearts.

So that was the worst season, without doubt the closest I've come to leaving. But even now I wish that I didn't have to work at marriage so much all the time. I wish everything were easier. But there's just no vacation for a marriage. I've had to do some hard work on myself; we both have. I've had to really look at myself.

I read a story of a man, an Iraqi, who was hunted by Saddam Hussein. In order to preserve his life this man built a space between the walls of his mother's home and hid there. He lived in that tiny place with only a mat to sleep on, his radio, and the Koran for nearly twenty years. He emerged only when Saddam was defeated. Imagine his shock when he looked in the mirror. He'd gone into hiding as a young adult and emerged a middle-aged man.

That's how I felt when I saw my image in the mirror of marriage—shocked at my true reflection. It was not how I thought I looked.

I saw myself in that mirror, but then I created a distorted reflection, even into my own mind too. It sounds peculiar, but it's almost like catching a glimpse, thinking, *Surely that isn't me,* but refusing to look again just so I can't be proven wrong.

If I didn't look back into that mirror again, then the image I was so unhappy with would no longer be there—or so I told myself. Kind of like when you think something may be physically wrong with you and you don't go to the doctor because what you don't know can't hurt you.

It sounds illogical, but most of us are ostriches at some time.

And so I'd go to God and pray and still deny the part of myself that I knew needed work. It seems foolish, but, yes, I tried to hide my true self not only from myself but also from God. I went before God and closed my eyes tight and hoped my sin would go away. I was like a little child who plays peekaboo; when the child closes her eyes, she thinks no one can see her anymore.

How original is that, anyway? How funny that I always thought it odd that Adam and Eve hid from God after they sinned. As if God wouldn't notice they were missing! I mean, what were they thinking?

By the same token, that's why I think God asked Jacob's name when Jacob wrestled with God. It was as if God was saying, *Tell me who you really are. Now, I know who you are, but you need to know, and you need to be honest about that before me. None of this coming to me in self-righteousness.*

Well, I guess at least I know I'm in good company with my self-righteous denial. I was reading the Psalms recently and noticed how David laments his sinfulness and admits to God what a wretch he is; then later he almost seems to justify his

83

shortcomings, saying that he knows he's not perfect, but then no one is, so God shouldn't be so hard on him.

So, realizing that I've been playing this game with God and with myself, I've looked again into the reflection that marriage has been forcing me to see. I've looked at the reality of who I am, and I've told God what I've seen—really seen.

I wish I could say that's the end of the story, that after my honesty with God and myself I've completely changed and become a new person. Well, I've made progress, and God is working on me, but I still fall into my natural tendencies. My eyes will always be blue. My husband and I will still have our obstacle that we can't seem to tear down permanently.

The one difference is I know that I'll keep trying, and he'll keep trying, and we'll have many more seasons. We still have to do some backbreaking snow shoveling in winter. But then spring arrives, and the ice thaws, leaving the ground wet as the sun glints overhead and enables us to see our reflection together, and we sparkle in the mirror created by the melted snow.

It's been said that a marriage that lasts has stood the test of time, but I don't think that time is a test. Time is a gift—a gift because change, growth, and compromise don't happen quickly. They come with time, and you've got to have time to work things out.

Today, as I look over the seasons we've been through in marriage, I see how far my husband and I have gone. At times we still fight over the same issues, and our arguments sometimes seem like déjà vu that's lasted twenty-one years, but I know we've come a long way. We needed time. For surely seasons are just that: our human way of making the passage of time tangible, the only way we can see something so abstract.

I like what I see through these blue eyes of mine.

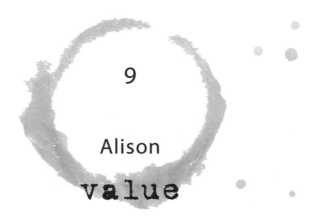

9

Alison

value

It's not beauty, but fine qualities, my girl, that keep a husband.

Euripides

I remember as a little girl daydreaming about being the most beautiful woman in the room. Whenever I saw an attractive woman, I would study her so carefully, my eyes memorizing every detail, as if watching her close enough would make me just like her. At home I never tired of watching my mom put on her makeup every morning. I begged her to let me wear it long before she gave in.

Today I can't even think about the money I spend each month on my appearance: hair color, haircut, eyebrow wax, bikini wax, manicure, pedicure, gym membership . . .

Don't we all want to feel attractive and know that others find us so? What is it that makes all women, across the span of time and country, want to be beautiful?

Glance at all the magazines in the grocery store checkout line. Eight out of ten feature glossy covers of beautiful, flawless people. Inside is news about beautiful people, advice about being beautiful, and page after page of products endorsed by beautiful people . . . all so we can be beautiful.

Walk down any metropolitan city street and you'll find women of all shapes, sizes, and ages dressed in suits, jeans, mini skirts, running shoes, high heels, designer labels, thrift store buys, ball caps, or pearls. Each woman is unique, each wants to be attractive to someone, and each yearns to pass the test of the toughest critic of all—herself.

I heard a story some time ago that I've been unable to forget—a story about a woman who suffered a very tragic past. She was beaten by her husband repeatedly, then her children were removed from her care because she "endangered" them by allowing them to live in a house with an abusive and danger-ous man. This offense, combined with an immigration dispute, landed the woman in jail for six months.

In the meantime, she suffered the indefinite loss of her children, who were parceled out among foster homes where they met one unspeakably abusive situation after another.

Eventually she was released from jail, was able to secure a job, and was in the process of trying to get her kids back. During this time, at a women's Bible study that often doubled as group therapy, the woman recounted one particular morn-ing when she'd caught the subway to work. She described climbing into the subway, feeling as though she'd been to hell and back. But here she was, thanks to the help of a local church, en route to a new job, wearing a brand-new dress—her first in years—and with hair styled and neat. There was much she was thankful for, yet all she could think about was the woman seated across from her. The stranger was well dressed and beautiful, at least in this beholder's eyes.

As the embattled woman described this moment, the silence from the other women in the Bible study became even more pronounced. They listened intently as this woman said she could not stop watching the beautiful stranger. Every woman in the room understood what was voiced in that moment—the desire to be as beautiful as that stranger.

The woman riding the subway to her new job hadn't wished for a nice home or larger bank account, for the pain of her past to be relieved, for the memory of abuse to fade away forever. She only wished for beauty. All the horror of her life so far—horror that had separated her to some degree from the experiences of the other women in her Bible study—suddenly faded. At the heart, every woman in the room was a kindred soul.

That is the power of beauty. No matter the means—for what is considered beautiful changes with time—our end is the same. We are captive to the power of beauty because beauty is power.

I'll be honest, it feels incredibly good when I can tell in the eyes of a stranger that he thinks I'm attractive. After all, attractive people, both men and women, can get things. I became used to getting what I wanted—not that I tried to use my appearance to manipulate, but little exceptions were made for me all along. As I got older and started dating, this really became apparent to me.

The power goes back the other way too. Why can someone I don't even know look at me, and then look again, and I instantly feel ten feet higher? That person is no one in particular to me, they don't know my name, who I am, what I do, what I think about. Yet I allow them to contribute to my sense of value. I can stay "high" off of that all afternoon. And sadly I put much of my value as a person into feeling beautiful.

Looking back, I realize that much of my self-esteem and value came from my looks. I didn't consciously connect the two, but I got a greater amount of attention from people, and men in particular, based on my appearance. Of course this made me feel like a better person. What woman doesn't feel flattered when a man behaves appreciatively toward her?

Because of this incredible boost of confidence that attention from others gave to me, I loved to be pursued by men and loved the way it made me feel. I was enthralled by this feeling, only I didn't realize this until I was married.

When I met my husband, his attraction to me was no different than any other guy I'd dated. But he wasn't intimidated by the fact that many others pursued me as well. He fought for me and wooed me.

I had a high demand for the romantic, and he fulfilled my needs. You remember how that is—the joy, the sheer adrenaline you feel when being pursued. You wait for every phone call, almost willing the phone to ring, and then feel the rush of delight when it finally does. There are the flowers, romantic dinners, and poetry—yes, poetry. There's the way he looks at you . . . who doesn't feel gorgeous, sexy, interesting, and desired during that time? How I wish I could bottle that feeling up!

But I was equally crazy about my husband, and so I eagerly married him, after dating only five months. I promised to love him and forsake all others. Everyone promises that, but only after being married for a while would I realize that there was much work to be done inside of me if I was going to keep my promise. Most people think that it's men who struggle with having to be with one person for the rest of their lives after committing to marriage. But I, as a woman, deeply struggled with knowing that it would have to be enough for me to have the attention of only one man—forever. Behind my attractive exterior, there was a part of myself that I was seeing for the first time.

After we married I really struggled to feel attractive and valued. I know that those aren't synonymous, but they were to me, sadly.

Though I knew my husband was very attracted to me, he was only one man. Was it enough? Was I really to spend the rest of my life being appreciated by only one man? It wasn't appropriate to flirt with other men as I had before I was married, so I stopped actively vying for their attention. But inside I still craved it. And because this desire was so connected to my identity and self-esteem, I questioned my value at the inherent loss of attention from others that comes with marriage. And my husband didn't seem to woo me as he had before.

Oh, I know it's normal, and I think it happens to the majority of couples, but after he "captured" me he seemed to take it easy. The days of flowers and little surprises "just because" were fast becoming faded memories.

Still, I knew I needed to enjoy and appreciate the security of being for my husband only. I needed to find excitement and contentment in his affection and approval, and I knew I needed to restore my value as a woman to its rightful place. I have loved being a woman and am full of pride for our gender and all our diverse beauty—beauty that is not limited by age, hair color, skin color, weight, or height. So it was not that I wanted to shed my desire to be beautiful, it was that I needed to move this desire to a place in my life where it belonged.

But how do you do that?

Unsure how to proceed but knowing I needed to do something, I turned to my Bible and began to meditate industriously on 1 Peter 3:4, which talks about the unfading beauty of a gentle and quiet spirit.

The unfading beauty of a gentle and quiet spirit.

Now, okay. I have to be honest here. That idea sounds so unappealing—boring, bland, Victorian—like something only unattractive people need. Maybe it's just because in our society many perfectly good words have been hijacked, and we've lost the truth of their original meaning. For instance, I've been to enough "estate" sales to know that this is one word that doesn't mean what it used to ("resort" is another word I'd never trust now to mean what was originally intended). So when "quiet and gentle" translated to me as "silent and meek"—two words that I'm not, nor ever will be—I continued to search for meaning.

I substituted my own word that contains the same idea—sweetness. Maybe the spirit of 1 Peter 3:4 is sweetness, which to me means kindness, grace, and goodness.

More than pleasing my husband or the masses, after all, I truly did want to be pleasing to God. And I have learned that the most beautiful thing I can have is a sweet spirit. The thing is, I haven't just theoretically traded the exterior beauty for an interior one. Sure, we all know that beauty is on the inside, as they say. And I truly believe that. We all know people who have become more attractive as we've gotten to know them better. But even though we believe that what is on the inside is what matters, we still want an attractive outside. Beauty is from God, I believe, and he created woman brilliantly. So I'm not saying that beauty doesn't matter, and to say that it's only the inside that counts is something that, even if true, is very hard to live by. If I tried to say that this is all that matters to me, my words would not be genuine. External beauty does matter to me, and I think it always will.

But what's in the soul is a beauty that will transcend time and circumstance. I live in that knowledge now. And more important, I know that beauty is not what gives me value. It can vanish in an instant, and even if it doesn't, time will assuredly change the landscape of my face and my body.

I definitely still love clothes and makeup, I hope I will always take care of my appearance, and I'd be lying if I said it doesn't still feel good when a man does a double take. But the amazing thing is this: when I know I'm wearing the garment of a sweet spirit, I feel my most womanly, my most beautiful, and my most confident about who I am and where I am.

10

Natalie

acceptance

Marrying a man is like buying something you've been admiring for a long time in a shop window. You may love it when you get it home, but it doesn't always go with everything else in the house.

Jean Kerr

Before I left for work this morning, I walked through my house and tidied everything. My eye took in every detail as I made sure nothing was out of place. Before I closed the front door behind me, I looked back once more to check that everything was just so.

When I returned home tonight, fatigued after a long day, I felt immediately calmed to see everything just as I'd left it: neat, orderly, and in its place.

That's me—extremely fastidious. Even as a child I never had to be told to clean my room. A bona fide perfectionist, I've always liked things organized and tidy. Perhaps it's my way of controlling my environment in order to feel more control over my life. But does it sometimes seem as if control freaks are magnets for eventual messiness, as if they are a lightning rod in an electrical storm?

In seven years with my husband I've learned that relationships and people aren't always neat and orderly. In fact, they can be quite messy—and I don't mean that he leaves clothes lying around. Fusing together two fallen people with their emotions, hurt feelings, past regrets, human frailty, and unrealistic expectations is not always pretty, nor is it always neat and contained.

One of the greatest things I've learned so far has been that I have to accept this whole person whom I have married.

Of course, my upbringing, and the contrast of it to my husband's, made this acceptance difficult. I was raised in a very conservative Christian home. An only child, I went along with everything and had very little conflict with my parents. I was rarely disciplined, not because I was spoiled, but because I rarely needed to be.

My husband, on the other hand, came from a very different family. He wasn't raised in a Christian home. His parents were divorced, and he didn't have much of a relationship with his father. His teenage and college years were checkered at best. A bit of a wild child, he was a late bloomer and took a while to come to a place where he was able to settle down and marry.

When we first met, his family greeted me with open arms, no questions asked. It didn't matter where I came from or who

I was. They were going to love me no matter what—and love me, they certainly have.

Then there were my parents. Upon meeting this man their daughter had fallen head over heels for, they grilled him for hours and discussed relentlessly the psychological disposition of his family members and the effect on us and our future children. I was mortified. Why did they make my husband-to-be feel so inadequate, especially when his family had been so welcoming of me?

My parents publicly gave us their blessing but privately gave me the feeling I'd chosen badly.

Until this point, they'd made all the other choices in my life for me. So I wondered, *Are they unhappy with my choice of a husband simply because they didn't choose him first?*

Despite the fact that I was embarrassed by their treatment of my husband when we were dating, soon after we got married I realized that I was casting my own judgment on him. I wanted to organize him into little compartments like I organize my closet or my accessories drawer. I found myself discarding the things I deemed "unwearable" or out of style, instead keeping only the glamorous and outwardly impressive pieces of him. I never liked mess and wasn't prepared to deal with the messiness that his past, and even my own upbringing, would bring to our world.

My parents had a very strong marriage. That was the model for me—a committed and harmonious relationship—and it was a good one. But I was very sheltered, and I wish they'd talked more about their mistakes and about the struggles in relationships and human nature. I'd never seen relational messiness before, and I was at a loss as to how to rein it in and find a place for it. Nothing was fitting where I thought it should.

Into the first year of our marriage and after many battles, we entered the throes of a full-on conflict. Anger seethed from him, panic from me, and incidentally our conflict resolution was as bloody as a civil war and about as effective as a treadmill as a method of transportation.

It all seemed so unmanageable. Impossible.

So we swallowed our pride and slinked to our premarital counselor's office. I might as well have looked both ways before ducking in the door. Someone might see us and know our marriage was less than perfect. But I could no longer wear a disguise. Though we both were prideful, we were desperate for help.

Sadly, and I'm sure for numerous reasons, the counselor did not help us. I was bawling my eyes out as the time came to a close. We'd uncovered a lot of grime and flung plenty of dirt and then were sent out of the counselor's office in a total mess, tear-streaked and still covered in the mud we'd just hurled at each other the last hour. Our counselor, who was also our pastor, didn't seem to have the time to see us again right away, and we were severely wounded by his lack of care for us.

Here we were up to our eyeballs in grime, and we felt as if he'd just shoveled on another load.

As a result we ended up leaving our church for two years. I eventually continued to go, but only to maintain appearances, and it was a further point of tension that my husband refused to go with me.

I don't know why, but it seems so easy to blame God and his entire church when a handful of Christians, in this case just one, do us wrong. When someone we hold in such high esteem spiritually lets us down, their fall from the pedestal can crush beyond recovery the worshipers below. And it doesn't make logical sense, but lashing out at anyone who shares any similar characteristics with that fallen hero seems to temporarily assuage the disillusionment—guilt by association, I guess. And maybe we think that if they knew the depth and breadth of the hurt they caused us, they would be forever plagued by guilt, or maybe we think that constructing a wall will protect us from further hurt.

In our situation, leaving the church and casting away anyone to do with it only hurt us more. Now we were left to figure out this thing alone. We made a complete disaster of everything, as if both of us were two storms colliding and destroying each other. The perfect storm, but that was just it: it was so un-perfect. I was drowning in a sea of sludge.

I had friends who were married, but they never talked about their marriages. I had one friend who I thought might understand, but I could never bring myself to talk to her about it because she never got that transparent with me. So my husband and I pressed on no matter the destruction and tried to work through our problems, but to no avail. At one point he suggested divorce, and truthfully, it was only the idea of how embarrassing a divorce would be that kept me from agreeing.

Finally, and miraculously, my husband released his bitterness toward our pastor and forgave him enough to at least go back to see him. I don't know what came over my husband, except that it was just God. He made an appointment with the man we still saw as our lifeline despite the deep hurt he'd caused us. That was the long-awaited break in the storm, and we started to go to him on a regular basis and work through all that churned within us as individuals and as a couple.

Over the years I've learned to accept my husband for who he is: his past, his present, and even who he may become. Though I'm not a part of his past, I must accept it, knowing I have the gift of being in my husband's present and future.

Am I still a neat freak?

Of course! I still have to fight the mind-set to try to clean up my husband. But I'm learning to edge out of my comfort zone, and I see how underneath my tidy façade I'm just as messy as he is. We're both a mess, and we both can go to God still covered in dirt because God is like a custodian. Not only does he clean my filthiness, but he's not concerned about the mess. He uses our marriage as soap.

I don't know if we'll ever be polished to perfection here together. Maybe. Maybe one day we'll have all these issues figured out. Until then, every time I get dismayed over a mess, I try to remember that even in the streaks and film God still sees his reflection.

11

Olivia

faithfulness

Like everything which is not the involuntary result of fleeting emotion but the creation of time and will, any marriage, happy or unhappy, is infinitely more interesting than any romance, however passionate.

W. H. Auden

Remember the way your heart beats fast when the person you've had your eye on all evening looks your way and your eyes meet? Remember the agonizing ecstasy of wondering whether or not he's actually interested in you as you look for a sign in everything he says and does or doesn't do? Or the on-top-of-the-world confidence you feel when a guy flirts with you, when he's attracted to you and you know it, that spine-tingling anticipation waiting for him to walk into a room? What about the way your stomach plummets all the way to your toes when his fingertips accidentally brush the bare skin on your arm? Or the electricity in a first kiss, and that literal weak-in-the-knees feeling . . .

They are powerful feelings that become sweet memories.

To say yes to marriage, yes to commitment and the man I chose to love and our life together, forever, is to say no to all those magnificent firsts and the exhilarating yet tortured angst that comes with a new relationship. I guess you trade all that for true intimacy, for safety and security. Rather than exhilaration, it's like coming home, and yet . . . was I ever much of a homebody?

I never imagined myself as one who would be unfaithful in marriage. In fact, I always considered loyalty to be one of my best traits.

When I met my husband, I was sure he was the one. We dated for less than a year and had a very short engagement. I never looked back. I loved him, loved romance, and looked forward to marriage—a longed-for dream being realized.

Now I've been married for almost ten years, and it's been good so far. We're comfortable with each other. Sure, there are the usual ups and downs, adjustments, fights, making up, learning to live with each other—forever. My husband is a wonderful partner and good friend. But I feel that I still have many unmet needs. Maybe we're inherently incompatible. He doesn't seem to know just what I need when I'm sad or frustrated; most of all, he doesn't seem to understand me when I crave understanding more than anything.

My heart doesn't pound the way it used to when we were first dating. It used to be that his just taking my hand had the effect of a roller coaster. You know that feeling of excitement that seems to overtake your entire body? Well, it's gone. What's replaced it is just an easiness.

That and now a certain excitement about another man who has unwittingly entered my life and turned my world on its side. I fear that this new man may be my soul mate. He is everything my husband is not, meaning that this other man is like me in all the ways my husband and I are different. We can talk forever about our mutual interests. I feel a connection with him both in our everyday interests and activities as well as in the depths of our minds and souls—the things we think about, struggle with, desire to talk about. He's so incredibly smart and well read. He stimulates my mind. We agree on so many issues, and the ones we disagree on generate wonderful, lively discussions. Our differences, in fact, stimulate me rather than threaten my ideas and intelligence. We can disagree, and all the while he's respectful of my opinions.

He seems to take in every detail of who I am, to notice the things no one else ever seems to—as if he's the first one who's ever truly gotten me.

I've fallen in love with a million things about him. What especially attracts me is the way he treats others, the way he's kind to everyone. I've seen him converse with young and old, and he treats them all with respect and sincere interest. He's simply exciting in every way.

The thing is, I have no good reason to believe he has any of these same feelings for me. No romance has passed between us, though I feel electricity surge through me when I'm near him. Those times aren't frequent. I watch him from afar and work at relating to him only as a friend. My blood rushes just to see him, though. My hands shake, and I'm sure he can hear my heart pounding.

The truth is, I think about nothing but him, and my heart truly breaks because I will never be with him. I hate even now every woman who will come into his life in the future. When he talks about other women, I'm pierced with jealousy. I cannot stand the thought of someone else getting to have him when I cannot.

I'm desolate because I don't know how I can be content in my life anymore. So this is what heartbreak feels like . . .

What if he is my soul mate? Do I believe there is such a thing? I never thought I did. But now . . . If soul mates do exist, am I to miss out—to live my life knowing that I must walk away from my one soul mate because I found him too late, because I took a wrong turn?

I do feel that I deserve this, deserve true love and passion— that everyone does. Yet to be with another man is morally wrong. There's no loophole for this. My contract in marriage is forever binding not just with my husband but with God, until he releases it. I have no option but to forget this other man.

Besides, I could never hurt my husband this way.

The world would definitely say I should do what makes me happy, that I deserve to be happy. But doesn't my husband deserve happiness too? In this situation, it seems that we cannot both be happy at the same time. I don't even have to open my Bible to know that Jesus did not come into the world so I could be happy. I was not created by God to make myself happy. And nowhere in the Bible is there a get-out-of-jail-free card for whoever meets their soul mate after they've married.

So if I believe what it means to be a Christian, then I must believe that I'm here to glorify God and enjoy him, not necessarily to simply enjoy the fruits of life and be happy.

It's so hard to die to desire, though—and much harder to enjoy God when he's so far away without a tangible presence. Harder yet because this other desire, this man, is right here in the flesh. Which leads me to wonder: does God really care how fulfilling my marriage is for me?

When I look at many of the marriages in the Bible, it doesn't seem as though they meet any other needs than sex for the man and bearing children for the woman. Sarah, Rachel, Leah—each one of them was eager to hand over her maidservant to be with her husband just so she could lay claim to a child. There is no way a woman would do that today. Women are hardly charitable with each other when it comes to sharing men. Where did we get the model for marriage that we have today? Where did we get romance and the idea of soul mates? Is it even possible for most people? Are we searching for the pot of gold at the end of the rainbow? Is it conceivable that at twenty-two years old someone can choose a mate whom they will still want at eighty-two?

No. At least not if I'm looking for a marriage just to meet my own needs. Who knows all their needs at twenty-two, anyway?

I didn't.

Maybe the point is that God does. Maybe he wants me to finally believe that he's leading and guiding me in the decisions I make and that he'll give me the grace to sustain my commitment.

Can God make my heart follow where my head says I must go? Can he make my desires instantly disappear? I know he can, so why, so often, doesn't he?

I've prayed that eventually my emotions, my heart, will catch up with my head. I prayed and prayed and prayed for release from these feelings. And for my own sanity, I've come to the conclusion that I must never see this other man again. In some ways it seems that he's backed away from me too, though I can't be sure. It's not something I can put my finger on; it just seems as though when I see him now, a wall has gone up that was put there for emotional survival.

I still think about him, not every minute, but just when I think I've succeeded in nearly erasing him from my mind, my dreams at night betray the truth in my heart. I awake to fresh sadness in the unkind light of morning. So, the feelings linger . . . and yet I've come to a new place.

There are things I know now. I know that this passion, this other man as my perfect soul mate, isn't real, at least not the way I've made him to be. All the things I feel for this man are just that—feelings, and feelings never put to the test. The head rush, the tingling in the pit of my stomach, these aren't reality either, at least not a sustainable reality. I see now that I imagined a relationship and juxtaposed what was only imaginary onto what is real. In the imagined relationship, all is perfect. We sit by the water at dusk or before a crackling fire or under the soft blue of moonlight—anywhere that casts a magical glow of light. We talk and relate, and he validates my every thought, every feeling. It's as if music is playing, and we practically ride off into the sunset. Never mind that I'm allergic to horses. In these imaginings, that doesn't seem to matter. If these dreams were a movie, the abrupt scratch of a record or squeal of a soundtrack would be interrupting right about now, because that's exactly what all this is—silver screen dreams, a fantasy.

I'm not minimizing the effect this man's had on me. So many of the things I like—no, love—about him are indeed real and wonderful. But we've never had to survive real life or routine together. How can the stark black and white of reality ever hope to compete with the golden hue of dreams?

In reality, my husband and I drag ourselves out of bed every morning to the obnoxious buzzing of the alarm clock. We fight traffic on the way to work and get stopped at every light. We're so busy during the day that we only have time to talk about who can be home when the cable guy comes or what's for dinner or what time to pick up the kids from school or how much the repair bill is for the car. In real life we get in bad moods, hurt each other's feelings, pay bills, go over budget, let each other down, act selfishly, have limited time for recreation—and we're tired, so very tired. In real life, dreams get broken; there are misunderstandings, annoyances, and grievances. Passion gets stale.

But what's also real is the way my husband tells me he loves me before we go to sleep every night; the way he tries so hard to choose a gift for me (even though he just doesn't get it right); the way he still looks like a little boy with his hair standing on end when he first wakes up in the morning; or the way he gets the oil changed in my car without a reminder or question. What's real is the way he rubs my back when I've had a tough day, or talks about me with pride to our children, or gets mad for me when I tell how someone hurt my feelings; the way he tries to make me happy in a million little ways; and the way we looked into each other's eyes and promised each other and God to stay together and forsake all others. It's real, I remind myself, the way he's seen me at my worst, my real worst, and still wants to spend the rest of his life with me, in sickness or in health; and the way I know, without a doubt, that I could be physically disfigured and he would still think I'm beautiful.

That's reality, and I guess that's *home*.

What grounds this reality is something I've been thinking on long and hard, the idea that if I believe marriage was created in part to illustrate God's relationship with his people (and I do believe that), then I have to look at the ebb and flow of my relationship with him.

Thinking back to earlier times in my life, I was on fire for God, passionate and fearless. What happened to my fearlessness?

There have been times when I've felt God's silence, or when my expectations of him and my prayers have met disappointment, or when I've tried spending time with him and don't know what to say, or when I've believed that living a certain way would honor him yet it's really, really hard. If I'm honest, I admit there are times when my passion for God has become musty and old.

Still, my relationship with God today is far deeper and more mature than my relationship with him in my younger years—richer, more textured, more honest. Even though my affection and attention are often seduced by other things, I still persevere and pursue my relationship with him. I do this because it's right and true.

I don't know if this is the last time I'll ever fall for someone else. I don't think my heart can take it. I certainly didn't go looking for it this time, and it has tortured me so; it still does at times. And I still don't know if soul mates really exist and if I had to walk away from mine. But I do know God is sovereign over my life. He has a plan for me, and has all along.

I've realized that, sure, home isn't always exciting; it can even be flat-out mundane at times. A lot of times. And often I just don't feel like the mundane. Most of us don't. But I guess it's up to us—the two of us, my husband and I—to keep it interesting, to work at it. I know we'll need a lot of help, but we will sustain it.

12

Susannah

friendship

There is no more lovely, friendly, and charming relationship,
communion, or company than a good marriage.

Martin Luther

Today I cleaned my house in one of those moods where I
actually enjoyed it. The feeling was more than just the joy of
being around the house or accomplishing something. Today I
took in the detail of each room, judging each decorative item,
each picture frame, every lamp, even my photo albums, as
I dusted.

One album in particular stole my attention, the one from
college showing me with my roommates, old boyfriends, and
best friends hanging out in our dorm rooms, at parties, and on
road trips. Tucked in the back were a few special letters from
friends I'd kept. I opened up each one and was filled with a
tidal wave of nostalgia that threatened to sweep me away. I

plunged in to read more. Instantly submerged in the past, I sat down on the hardwood floor, planning to linger a while. I had no schedule to keep today, so I savored the extra time.

At the bottom of the stack was a letter from my best friend, written at the time of my graduation. Her small, neat handwriting chronicled our many adventures in a way that only she could: she took me back to late-night talks when we were so tired we continued our conversations with eyes closed, to moments of shared confidences, to small joint acts of rebellion as we both tried out our freedom, to personal triumphs or failures, and to that total codependence that just feels so safe, so secure, and so eternal. I mean, your parents have to love you, but others don't, so those best-friend relationships were always so special to me, giving me a much-needed boost of confidence as well as a partner in crime and a soul companion. My best friend and I still talk occasionally over the phone, and more often by email. But she lives in another state, has a family and responsibilities that eat up her time—and so do I.

Oblivious to the hardness of the floor underneath me, I leaned back against the closest space of wall not cluttered with furniture, still in my reverie. For a few moments I wanted to go back to that place and time, even though it was a roller coaster. We were discovering who and what we were meant to be; we were cheering on and clinging to each other for dear life when the hills got steep or we were turned upside down and thrown for a loop. *Why do things have to change?* I wondered. *Why do boys get in the way? Why do we grow up and move on?* Now instead of the comfort of our best friends we have husbands, families, jobs, mortgages, car payments . . .

Isn't this what we said we always wanted? Isn't this what more than half of our long talks were even about?

So where do friends fit in with a marriage?

I'd always wanted to marry and planned on it, but I knew it wasn't going to happen quickly. When I became a Christian at twenty-three, I radically changed the type of man I was looking to marry. But I'd come from a more decadent past, so now that I was determined to marry a Christian man, there weren't many around who didn't seem weird or boring, at least compared to guys I'd previously known.

Meanwhile, I lived my life to the fullest. Unlike many women who seem to put their lives on hold while waiting for a husband, I charged ahead with my career and enjoyed relative success. I had dear friendships, best friendships, and these were very emotionally fulfilling. The only thing lacking in my life was sex, and I sure did miss that! Still, when the man I was to marry came along, I was a little reluctant to give up my singleness. I liked it; I truly enjoyed being on my own and the independence it afforded me.

So I corresponded with this man platonically for two years.

Truthfully, in spite of my reluctance to commit and to give up my freedom, sexual desire won out. I realized I wasn't meant to be alone. My husband was a wonderful man, so gentle, kind, and patient—the exact opposite of me. He was intellectually equal to me, however, and I respected him, and that was vital. We finally moved our friendship into a dating relationship, and after a four-month official courtship, we married.

109

I was twenty-nine years old, and my expectations of marriage were simple. I only wanted two things: commitment (since I'd grown up in a broken home and insisted that mine would be a marriage that lasted) and friendship—an enduring and deep friendship. I envisioned long talks, the exchange of ideas, the freedom to share my deepest thoughts, dreams, and fears, all of which I was sure would be understood. In fact, I imagined my husband would understand me so well that I wouldn't need to finish my thoughts at all. He would just get me. After all, my girlfriends had—and if marriage was to be more intimate and forever, then why wouldn't I expect this kind of blending of soul, heart, and mind?

So not only did I expect that understanding in marriage, but I also assumed I'd always feel loved and complete, as in a friendship, only . . . *more.* I was sure there would be nothing we couldn't talk about, share, and understand.

And that's just how it was.

Yeah, right. It's probably no surprise that I was severely disappointed. My husband didn't understand me at all. Sure, he listened and made an effort, but not only did we have the gap of gender communication (those differences alone made me feel we were from different universes), but we were such completely opposite individuals too. Where I was opinionated, he was open-minded. Where I was outspoken and brash, he was silent and methodical. Where I was adventurous and free, he was cautious and wary.

Plus, there was this one thing I never expected: the closeness of our lives, the intertwining of our lives together, forever, actually seemed to hinder our intimacy.

I thought building a life together would drive us to unparalleled closeness. Rather, I was threatened, felt insecure, and realized it was easier to fully open up to a friend who ultimately didn't drive the course of my life. It was less risky to confide in a friend, because no matter how great my best friends were, I didn't stand to lose as much if they rejected me or if I didn't take their advice or agree with their opinions. In friendship, I remained in control.

Not so with my husband. This man could either make better or ruin the rest of my life. When he expressed an opinion different than my own, I felt vulnerable and as if I was losing control over my life. I had a whole lot more to lose now, and it scared me. There's far more at stake when you intimately communicate with your spouse. The rejection I could face for something I said or didn't say, did or didn't do would be potently powerful. If he decided to abandon his faith or leave his career, those choices would have an enormous impact on my life.

The bottom line is that no matter how close I was with my friends, I had lower expectations of them and I gave them more freedom to be who they were. I didn't do this for my husband. I withheld grace from him and was threatened by his differences, quirks, thoughts, and desires. I guess it was kind of like backseat driving. I'm not in the habit of telling a car on the other side of the road which way to turn. Why do I care where they go? But the person driving my car? I have a personal interest in that one, and I usually make this known loud and clear.

Today, I'm in the twenty-sixth year of marriage, and in recent years we've finally begun to experience that deep, abiding friendship I'd always dreamed of. It's a beautiful place to be as a couple, but it's taken a long time to get here. I had to release my idea of what friendship with my husband was supposed to be, because he wasn't and never will be one of my girlfriends. I also had to loosen my grip a little on the friendships I'd already forged with others. I'd been holding so tight to those relationships that I wasn't letting my husband in; I wasn't allowing friendship to be unique to him and to us. I was too full with no room for him.

So my youthful friendships changed. They had to. I'll always look back on them with sweetness, and I look forward to my many close friendships with other women, friendships I wouldn't trade for anything.

But what I have with my husband has evolved into something so special, something shared uniquely by the two of us. We've come together in a way I'd never have thought possible or even really desired, five years ago. I've been able to tell him things I've never told anyone else, and I'm able to be truly myself and know he'll still love me, more even than when we got married.

As safe and secure as those other friendships once felt, this is safer.

I don't want to disparage my other friendships because those are a priceless treasure to me. But in opening myself up to friendship with my husband, I feel as if I traded in my costume pearls, lovely as they were, for real ones.

These are priceless.

And you know how to test a genuine pearl, don't you? You bite down on it and the luster stays, the strength is there. What you have is real.

13

Catherine

reconciling
the past

Men marry to make an end; women to make a beginning.

Alexis Dupuy

How much does our past affect our present and future? I wonder if it is something we can even quantify, though certainly there are always the experts and the "they" who try. It always bothers me when I hear someone lament the "baggage" their partner brought into the relationship. After all, we all have a past. We all bring baggage, it's just that some of us travel lighter than others. In part, we are all shaped by the experiences of our past. Our history affects the way we look at the world, how we perceive things, the goals we set, the dreams we chase, and the decisions we make. From a school bully, a caring teacher, our parents, and previous relationships, so many people and events that comprise our past will forever live in our future. So how do we keep scenes from the past from playing out like a crystal ball predicting the future?

My parents separated when I was two years old and then divorced when I was four. Though I know their divorce has forever shaped me—and it's certainly marked my marriage—I don't really remember much about that time, and most of what I do know has been reconstructed by well-meaning family members.

My grandmother, for instance, at least twice a year used to evoke the acrid memory of my dad leaving. Why she did this on a regular basis I still don't know, but I used to recoil when she got to the part about me in the sordid plotline. She told of my father leaving and of me, as a two-year-old child, clinging to his leg, crying for him to stay. She said my father peeled my tiny body off of him and passed me over to my mother.

It's a pitiful story, and I revolted to hear it every time because I hated the vulnerability, the categorical love of a child, the power of a man to hurt, and the ability to love so much yet know so little. And so even when I was very young, I promised never again to allow myself to be that vulnerable. As I grew older, this meant I entered relationships with my head, not my heart.

These feelings were reinforced by other events in my upbringing. My mother later remarried (I was thirteen at the time), despite promises that she would never choose someone we kids didn't love too. My stepfather was mean, at times cruel, and I saw my mother bow to that. I think she would say that submitting to her marriage has made it victorious, but all I see is a loss of her self-respect in the way my stepfather treats her. So, again, this time as a teenager, I saw vulnerability, and I loathed it.

My earliest understanding of sex was that it was bad, though I didn't really know what it was. My father had left my mother, left us, because he was having an affair. Even as a child I saw the affair for what it was—sex. I saw it as breaking up my parents' marriage, not as a potentially good thing in the correct context.

Because of the divorce, my mother worried about me and my sisters and our ability to be in a healthy relationship with a man. Out of fear and armed with statistic after statistic that she crammed into her mind (things like "75 percent of the children of divorce end up with serious psychological, social, or academic problems"), my mother forced us to read countless books in order to combat the negative impact of the divorce.

Sadly, I believe the negative impact became almost a self-fulfilling prophecy. I had sex in many of my relationships, but used sex for power not love. I cheated in my relationships. Maybe I was trying to hurt my boyfriends before they hurt me; maybe I was trying to reassure myself I could be attractive to someone else if my boyfriend rejected me. Whatever the reason, I behaved destructively in all of my dating relationships, not only toward the person I was dating but ultimately toward myself.

I know I married my husband for the wrong reasons. I thought making the status of our relationship right in the eyes of God would erase the sin and the shame I felt over not only this relationship but also previous ones too. I felt that as a Christian I was living a double life and that to marry would merge the two worlds—the one I was actually living with the

115

one others thought I was living—and then that would silence the noise in my head. I thought that our married life together would forever end the sin, the guilt, and every bad problem we had, and we would start a new and wholesome life being godly and in the end living happily ever after.

To look back on that now seems so foolish, and yet it was entirely true in my head. Marriage has been a lot more work than I ever anticipated. The cruelly ironic thing is that my husband had exactly the opposite expectations I did. When we married he thought the work was now done; he'd secured himself a wife, and the hard part was over. For him it was the end, and yet I thought it was just the beginning. Our views going into marriage were completely contrary to each other.

With the realization that my expectation for marriage isn't to be met, I've struggled these past years with trying to control things. I probably always tried to control things, but this desire for control became palpable to me in marriage as I saw myself trying to control the every thought of this other person. I tried to control everything he did, even his thoughts and feelings. I quickly passed judgment on anything he said or did that I felt he shouldn't. I was always trying to figure out not only what God was trying to do in my life but also what God was trying to do in his as well. Always pointing out where I felt there was a lesson for him to learn. I've felt that I should be the person seeing and interpreting what plan God had for both of us, judging what I feel God is doing or should be doing in the life of my husband. Maybe I was trying to make up for past sin by ensuring we walk the straight and narrow from now on, trying to make up for lost time. And I've struggled with the feeling that being married is like holding a magnifying glass up to my every flaw, and I really don't like what I'm looking at. How can I live with myself, let alone someone else?

The crazy thing is that I feel like a hypocrite even more than I did before my marriage. The one feeling I thought would be banished forever by marriage haunts me continually. People, like myself, have this idea that marriage is so much an entity that it becomes like a third person, a living and breathing person so strong as to overpower the other two people. But a white dress, a ceremony, and the pictures to prove it doesn't change who you are. You're exactly the same two people after you say "I do" as you were before.

That may sound like an elementary statement, but if it's so simple, why do people get married thinking it will change who they are or who the other person is? Rather, I've felt more duplicitous than ever, because now people think we have this perfect relationship when all the while I know how we fight and the things I say in anger and the scuffles we have. But it's all hidden behind closed doors.

I feel the demands of marriage are so enormous for me. There are times when there's nothing I want to do less than talk or when the last thing on earth I want to do is exactly what my husband wants. And as I do it I think, *If this isn't hard work, then I don't know what is.* Then there are the times when I don't do it, when I give in to the side of me that just thinks it's too hard.

There are days when I feel that I hate my husband and wish I could erase every day that we've spent together. I think it's difficult to be this way and be a Christian because Christians don't ever say those things or reveal that they think this way. Maybe they think it's un-Christian, or maybe they're worried about what people will think of them (oh, how much simpler

117

life would be for all of us if we never worried about what others are thinking!), or maybe they worship at the altar of marriage as I did—and to question the institution is to show lack of faith in our God.

There were many times I thought I wanted to give up on our marriage, times I couldn't stand the sight of my husband. I actually went for a long time thinking our marriage was a momentous mistake, especially whenever we fought. I'd automatically replay this internal tape: *I knew it. I did the wrong thing.*

Maybe I thought this way because of the example of my parents—two people unable to make a difficult marriage work—and my belief that the demise of my own union was lurking around the corner, waiting to pounce when I was weak. Then again, maybe I thought this way because I married for the wrong reasons, and that something that started wrong could never be made right, and that good could never come out of something that was as misguided as we were.

Whatever the reason, I convinced myself that my marriage was a blunder—the blunder of a lifetime.

In one sense this was freeing, to call a spade a spade. It relieved me of some of my responsibility and let me off the hook from having to work at my marriage. I reasoned that nothing I did was going to change the fact that this marriage was wrong.

But in a truer sense, my admission was damning. It was like sentencing myself to a life of mediocrity, imprisonment to a bad marriage, serving a lifelong sentence. And I did feel like a dead man walking. My hopes and dreams for my life were dying, and I grieved the loss more deeply than I would the death of a loved one.

So what do you do? I could just sit as our marriage collapsed around me, my eyes shut tight to keep the debris out. Or I could stand up, dust myself off, and walk away without even a backward glance. But when your vows tell you to stay, you can't just walk away, and so I fell into an abyss of depression.

Then one day a woman at my church approached me. She told me that she was praying for me and didn't want me to think my marriage was a mistake.

Who told you? I wondered immediately, both panicked and annoyed with this intrusion into my deepest thoughts. *How could you know?* I'd never told a soul, and I only ever saw this woman at church on Sunday mornings. Paranoid, I immediately wracked my brain for what I'd said or done that had betrayed my innermost thoughts. Had I dropped an unmeasured word and slipped with a facial expression? When every other head was bowed and every eye closed during prayer, had this woman somehow glanced up to see the tears that slipped down my cheeks before I could whisk them away?

Even days later, I couldn't shake our conversation. It haunted my thoughts and even irritated me. But I didn't know what else to do about it, so I began to pray—and to write.

In the process of such soul-searching I discovered something: my feelings of loss and mourning were true and real, but it wasn't the loss of the rest of my life that I was mourning. It was the loss of my expectations. In my darkest, deepest valley, the idol of marriage was defeated. I was left with something very real, not at all a fairy tale, but something both fallen and yet forgiving. From this earthy, ground-level place, I could only look up.

And I've also learned something else thanks to the mysterious woman I encountered at church that day. My husband and I aren't struggling out there alone. There are people who can come alongside us and who understand that marriage, even the best marriage, is hard. Such a precious gift, this gift of community! It reminds me that I'm not alone, that I'm not the only one messing up at this falling down business and then getting back up. Community reminds me that there are people in my life to brush off my knees when I fall, to bandage me up and send me back out to play.

That's when I see God's hand reaching out to lead me to a new place.

Taking hold of his grace has been my greatest triumph. It's meant getting past the fact that I thought my marriage was a mistake. It's meant taking captive every poisonous thought and instead appreciating the moment, the time my husband and I have now. True, I had rushed into marriage and didn't appreciate being single. But also true is how I can appreciate the time my husband and I have together, the way we've grown as people—and grown together.

How sweet it is, after all, to know and be known, to feel as though you can express your true self and be understood. This is what marriage affords: only my husband knows the true spiritual struggles I have. So much of my life is a façade—I can be so fake and hypocritical at work and church, unreal in the things I'm wrestling with. But my husband knows the truth; he knows my thoughts and weaknesses and angst—and it's okay. So with him, I'm real. And for me that is the culmination of everything I am—my past, present, and finally my future.

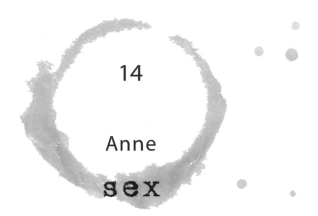

14

Anne

sex

Marriage is for women the most commonest mode of live-
lihood, and the total amount of undesired sex endured by
women is probably greater in marriage than in prostitution.

Bertrand Russell

Someone once told me that if sex in a marriage is good, it's
only about 10 percent of the relationship in terms of importance; if it's bad or a source of conflict, it's 90 percent. Well, I
wouldn't know if that's true, because it's only ever been one
way for me.

My husband and I were both virgins on our wedding night,
which meant sex was awkward, to say the least.

If you think about it, how could a first sexual encounter
not be awkward for couples who didn't have sex before marriage? It's a very strange mental and emotional phenomenon
that must take place.

First you go from having to train your will not to cross a certain boundary of physical intimacy. Yet leading up to marriage, you probably get to that line a million times and only by the grace of God do you stay strong. So you're tested on something countless times, and then, overnight, with the transition of a ceremony—a public one—all of a sudden that big Do Not Cross line in the sand is now gone. All that wasn't okay suddenly is encouraged and even expected.

Second, the night of the wedding is hardly the optimal first time for sexual intimacy. Truthfully, you and your bridegroom probably haven't seen much of each other all day. You've each been up since the crack of dawn working on every detail of your appearance—clothes, hygiene, demeanor, behavior—and you've been on the go all day since—this after months of detailed preparation. You suddenly realize you're exhausted and probably starved too. It's hardly the makings for the most romantic night of your life. So you get the point: it's awkward.

After our wedding day, when my husband and I entered our hotel room and the door closed behind us, instantly it seemed as if the issue of sexual intimacy was between us like a third presence. Like we both knew it was on the other's mind, but it felt so awkward. We had all these expectations of how it was supposed to be. But rather than romantic, it was a tension that felt palpable. Neither one of us wanted to talk about it. *But how to get started?* I didn't want to take off my beloved wedding dress. It was only a dress, I know, but I was sad knowing I'd never spend a day in it again. Sensing my nervousness, my husband suggested we take a bath together first. *Okay,* I thought, *that sounds like a good idea.* But I just wasn't ready for total nakedness yet. Imagine what he must have thought when I appeared in the bathtub wearing my bathing suit! Bless him, for he never said a thing about it, and he behaved as though everything was normal.

In the end our wedding night turned out okay. I'll never remember it as one of our better nights sexually, but I guess there is a sweetness to all that clumsiness too.

Now, sex is no longer awkward. Sure, there's still the occasional elbow in the eye or fumbling of buttons and ties, but we're much more routine now. We've been married too long for anything else.

What's interesting is I've never really enjoyed sex to the degree I imagined I would. Before we were married, I thought about sex all the time. I desperately wanted it and even boasted to close friends that my husband and I would have sex in every room and at least five times a week. But after marriage, sex just didn't hold the same allure. Almost all of my friends, most of whom are my age and have been married at least twenty years, say pretty much the same thing—they don't really enjoy sex. It's just something they do for their husbands, which lately has made me contemplate this whole human phenomenon called sex. Why does it seem so many married women don't enjoy it? What are we doing wrong? Could it be that everything we think about sex and women may be wrong?

This may be a radical question, but what if our perceptions of sex are wrong? What if somewhere in the beginning we got off track about sexual attitudes, expectations, and realities, and just passed on those misconceptions from generation to generation? What if we've been conditioning ourselves, raising sons and daughters with skewed perceptions of sex? What if the way women behave and think about sex is nurture, not nature?

I recall that as a young girl I was told to be careful about how I dressed and behaved around boys my age. Boys were prone to think about girls a certain way, I was told, and even though boys got off to a slow start before developing an interest in girls, by junior high they were going like gangbusters. Pubescent boys thought of nothing else but sex, and snapped girls' bras or hooted with laughter at the flash of a pair of girls' underwear. So girls were taught to take some responsibility here and try not to cause boys to stumble.

By high school and in the dating years, I was told I was going to have to take control of where a relationship went physically. Girls needed to draw the lines because boys were so sexually charged that it was too hard for them to do so. (And guys say we're hormonal!) I did take on that role. I drew the lines, and it was as difficult for me as I'd heard it was for the boys—really difficult. It wasn't made any easier with pressure from a boy either.

Then, as a young adult, when I started learning about marriage, I was taught that it's always the husband who's more motivated sexually. Women will want relational intimacy, and men will want sex. Women do tolerate sex in order to be good wives, often giving in to their husbands even when tired, stressed, or sick. We do this because we're told that this is what keeps a husband happy, home, and faithful.

And we buy into that. Think about it: how many women do we know who would say, "I don't love sex and never have"?

But what if we're just not meeting our sexual potential, the potential we were created for?

Why do I think that? Well, for starters, there's no doubt the human body is phenomenal, so expertly and purposefully designed. We believe our God is one of purpose and plan.

But do we know that the main pleasure-receiving body part of the female has no other purpose but to receive pleasure? It does nothing else. Nothing. It exists only to make us feel good. However, the same cannot be said of the equivalent male pleasure-receiving body part. That's right, theirs is of dual purpose.

Second, take a look in the Bible at the Song of Solomon. This book is held up as a biblical example of pure and true love and sexual attraction. Song of Solomon alludes to sex being for more than reproduction purposes. Sex is for a husband and wife, ready and willing. At one point in the book, the woman approaches the man, and it isn't just because she wants to make a baby. She wants him (and isn't it interesting that it's the husband who puts on the brakes and tells her "not yet"?). I don't know if he looked like Brad Pitt, but she appreciates a fine male specimen. She's attracted to his body and the way it looks and isn't just concerned about her emotional needs. And that's biblical!

Third, look at some current trends and culture. Who reads those trashy romance novels—the ones with Fabio-like men on the cover and some girl with a ripped bodice? A man wouldn't be caught dead with one of those paperbacks! The target market is women. A recent article by *Newsweek* magazine may indicate why: women are looking for sex too. In fact, the number of women seeking sex outside of marriage is growing and could possibly now equal the number of men who cheat.[3]

If all this is true, why do so many women not enjoy sex?

That's where I think the nurture issue comes in. We're raised to believe sex is about men's needs and that women have other, more important needs like emotional intimacy. In the late nine-

125

ties when the HBO original series *Sex and the City* premiered, it was considered radical, even to the secular world, because four women were talking openly about sex, aggressively going after sex, and having one-night stands—just like a man.

But here's what I think is the bigger problem. Men are taught the same thing about themselves and about women and sex. And I think because they are told that sex is more for them, even at a subconscious level, many men (though most certainly not all) don't make as much of an effort as they could to learn about the female body and make sure that sex is just as enjoyable for women. Men are told to cuddle afterwards because that fulfills a woman's emotional needs, and to be nice to her during the day or she won't be in the mood that evening . . . and that may be true. But isn't there more to it? What about plain old technique?

It's no secret that women are complicated, and not just emotionally so. Our bodies are more complicated than men's, and I think that many men—again, not all—don't really try to learn because they don't think it's important to us. To be fair, it's not really selfishness; it's just what they've been taught and the perception they've always been given. But women deserve amazing sex with their husbands just as much as the husbands do with their wives. Maybe, just maybe, if they had a taste of that, their view of sex would change.

Then, guess what, ladies? Our husbands wouldn't be able to keep up with us.

Now, all this is just my humble opinion. I'm not a doctor, a scientist, a historian, or a sex therapist. I'm certainly not saying that sex should be enjoyed outside the parameters that God has given either. I'm saying quite the opposite. I'm just a fiftysomething woman, happily married but unhappily having sex in what's supposed to be my sexual prime years, and I'm wondering if there's more to the story here than "his needs, her needs."

This whole little idea could be absurd, or I could really be on to something. If I am on to something, what could that mean for us?

Maybe it's time to find out.

15

Sandra

risk

The married are those who have taken the terrible risk of intimacy and, having taken it, know life without intimacy to be impossible.

Carolyn Heilbrun

My business is about taking calculated risks, and I'm good at it. I invest people's money for them—lots and lots of money. I'm not necessarily a bungee-jumping, sky-diving kind of girl, but just the same my work gets my heart beating faster, my mind racing, and my blood pumping—a fantastic feeling that reminds me that I'm alive. I live for it, this element of risk.

Without sounding like Chicken Little, I think we all do, to some degree, every day.

Given the statistics of vehicular accidents, every time I pull out of my garage I'm taking a risk, and so are you. Buying a house or a car, even raising children—all risks. Sure, they're calculated risks—the kind, like business transactions and important matters, that you rely on instinct before taking and even then support with facts, research, trends, and information. So what about the biggest risk of all? What about the risk of true intimacy and the commitment of "till death do us part"? Shouldn't that biggest risk, the one where you stand to lose the most, be the most calculated, the most informed, and the most sure?

I was raised in a very sad, dysfunctional family. My parents could have been so much more than they ended up becoming—they were both brilliant and talented. But my father was incapable of being faithful, and my mother, as if getting revenge, pursued her own infidelities. They were disinterested in their children and seemed to live only for self-destructive behavior—and this was the only behavior my sister and I saw modeled.

As I got older and became more aware of what was going on, I told myself I would never live like that. And I didn't. I became goal oriented. I finished college, then furthered my education and finally got a high-powered job. I'd achieved the success my parents had never achieved, and I was fulfilled in what I'd accomplished.

Both my parents passed away before I married, but it took many more years—and therapy—before I was able to forgive my father. I carried the hurt with me long after I'd left home and far into my adult years. I feared commitment, that maybe I or my husband wouldn't have what was required to remain faithful to one person forever. And I feared that I might be left one day, and that I would be left with nothing, no hope for the future and only squandered potential.

By the time I was brave enough to take the risk of loving a man, I was an almost thirty-year-old, independent woman who didn't feel the need to settle down. I worked long hours, socialized with interesting people at great parties, and had smart friends. I was like a turning disco ball, casting a ray of sparkle all around, and I finally chose to marry because I could anchor myself to this man. The man who would be my husband would stand strong and immovable, and I wanted that rootedness.

After living with my parents' behavior, I knew that to marry at all was the greatest risk I could take. I believed a good marriage was a full surrender, an invasion of myself—still, I was looking for support, friendship, and someone to come home to as well. I found all these things in my husband, and he loved me for my sparkle, the many facets I added to his life. To him, I was successful, exciting, and steady.

People would say to him, "Oh, you're the one who married Sandra," and that made him proud. He enjoyed the trail of glitter that followed in my wake.

The thing is, I was a new and impressionable Christian when we married. I had not been raised with religious values of any kind, and had no prior knowledge of what the Christian life required, so I accepted without question things I was told about how a Christian wife should behave.

I never could have anticipated how arduous the prescribed Christian life would be. Though I was used to thinking for myself, I simply submitted to the expectations of other believers. That included following what I was taught: that I should submit to the desires of my husband, not work outside the home, and not make decisions for us as a couple or even disagree with the ones that he made.

What a shock. I was educated, had lived on my own for quite some time, and knew I had a lot to offer our marriage. To suddenly not have any decision-making ability over my life didn't appeal to me at all. I didn't even know if I was physically capable of saying nothing when I disagreed.

Things erupted one day, which I still remember so vividly. I'd had the chance to participate in an event that I was so excited about, something very unique, a coveted opportunity. But due to a schedule conflict, my husband told me he didn't want me to participate. I was so deeply disappointed, but believing I was called to yield, I acquiesced to his wishes. And then I cried and cried for three days straight. Here I was, a willful, independent woman with a successful career, and all of a sudden I was to be silent?

My husband was stunned over how upset I was.

I took notice, real notice, of my life too. I knew I was more capable than this, that I had more to offer my husband than just blind submission. I began to look around at the other Christians I came in contact with, and all I saw was much unhappiness. Women, even smart, successful women, were hunting down the best men with the philosophy that they had one chance at this marriage thing, so they had to make the best choice. Because once married, if things didn't turn out as expected, they would have to suffer in silent self-torment. I saw how, in order to hold on to their men, these women reduced themselves to being voiceless and uninteresting.

There wasn't one couple I could look to as a healthy biblical role model. Was I, too, destined to be dreary and uninteresting like so many of the women I saw? I hoped not. I firmly believed it wasn't right for one person in a marriage to thrive at the expense of the other, and yet this is what I saw all around me. Joy, one of the fruits of the Spirit, seemed so absent.

What can I do? I wondered. I had come to a place of what I was told was proper submission in my marriage. Yet I couldn't possibly submit to the supposed rules that everyone I knew interpreted to be in the Bible and still be the unique woman God had created me to be. I was afraid. I've since realized how much we as women operate out of fear: we live in fear that we won't get married or that we'll marry the wrong person or that when we do find the right one he'll leave. I feared that if I stepped out of the mold I had been taught as a young Christian that my husband would leave me and God wouldn't honor me or our marriage. This fear wasn't based on my husband's thoughts and actions but on the formula I'd been shown for a safe marriage, a formula that went something like this: be the docile, meek woman meeting your man's every need, and this will secure your marriage.

And yet I no longer wanted a marriage like those others I was seeing. I was afraid of giving my husband that kind of power and control over me. But, at the same time, I was scared to step outside those parameters and explore for myself what God really intended. *How can that be?* I chided myself in self-talk. *I'm used to taking professional risks.* But this seemed different. I was afraid of ending up unhappy and losing who I was and all I could bring to this marriage. And I was a little nervous about giving God that much control too. What if he would do something I didn't want or like? (It's not that he didn't already have control, but there was something scary about admitting out loud that he had it.)

Then I reminded myself: *I haven't come this far in my life by not taking chances.*

132

And so I decided to experiment with fear, trust, and submission a little bit. I searched for something on which I could really test my faith—and it had to be something big, at least big enough so that later in my life, when I was trusting God in something else, I could look back and be reminded of how he answered me. *This isn't about testing God,* I reminded myself, *as much as testing myself and my ability to trust.*

That's when I knew just the area to begin my examination of marriage and faith, and how the two impacted each other. It would be in the area of having children.

When we were dating, my husband always said he wanted a big family; when we got married, we started having children right away. By this time in our marriage we had two children—and at two, I was finished. I never really wanted more than two kids, anyway. So I always secretly hoped my husband didn't mean what he'd said about a big family or that he'd change his mind when he saw how complete our family was with just two. I was sure he wouldn't want to mess with a good thing or that I could at least charm him out of those ideas. In fact, I was quite confident.

This was not the case. Though my husband loved our children dearly, they only made him want to have more. Just my luck. As much as I adored our children too, I didn't want any more. After all, I was the one who would have to go through another pregnancy and stay home with them. Shouldn't this be as much my decision as his?

Risky as it was, I decided to trust God to work out all for the good on this issue. I decided to give in to my husband and agree to have another child.

Obviously, for my first experiment in trust, I'd done considerably more than dip one toe in the water. I'd submerged myself! This was no little test. If God saw fit to give us a child, this was one experiment that would last forever. But I went with my gut and decided to risk big. After all, it wasn't my husband I was submitting to and trusting—it was God.

So, though I honestly didn't feel I could handle another child, I was trusting God to know what was best for me, even if his way differed from mine. I submitted to God, and I submitted to my husband's desires. And you know what? I never got pregnant. That was it. We never had more than two children. That was God's final answer, but not his final word, because what happened to me as a result was truly life changing.

My husband began to fully appreciate how I was willing to make sacrifices for him, and I came to a new realization about how much God really knows me. This was mind altering; it blew me away. *God knows me! He's created billions and billions of people, and yet he knows my individual needs, desires, and capabilities—and his purpose for me is always according to those needs.*

It certainly wouldn't be true to say that from then on I was the perfect submissive wife, nor was I the perfect submissive Christian. No, there was plenty more trial and error for both of us. But the resting place we came to as a couple came with time, and I grew in confidence.

Today I no longer fear that my husband will leave me. I know he's for keeps, and that gives me freedom to be who I am. Looking back, I wish I hadn't questioned so much of his judgment. And there are times when my husband wishes he'd followed my advice—like when I told him not to buy the house we're now trying to sell! Still, I think we balance each other, and we're interested in one another's goals. I never wanted to see marriage as limiting my dreams, and neither did he.

We're on a lifetime journey of pushing each other forward intellectually, relationally, and spiritually. We've taken risks together, and that makes life both exciting and interesting. I truly don't believe you can have a good marriage without taking chances together. We all know people for whom the ultimate risk, the risk of marriage, doesn't work out, but each day I learn to trust God with our marriage. He's in charge, even on the days when I question the choices, choices like where to send our children to school, a real estate deal, whether to sell or buy, how to balance our lives together. It sounds cliché. What does that really mean, right? But my husband and I know this to be true, and we know it in our hearts and souls and day by day.

Speaking of heart and soul, I never thought about the connection between faith and marriage before I was married. It didn't really occur to me that the two intersected so much. But marriage has allowed me to see Christ in a fuller way, to live without fear. Sure, the stakes are high, but my cards are on the table now.

16

Diana

idolatry

How many young hearts have revealed the fact that what they had been trained to imagine the highest earthly felicity was but the beginning of care, disappointment, and sorrow, and often led to the extremity of mental and physical suffering.

Catharine Esther Beecher

It's Halloween night, and the children in the neighborhoods are out in droves. Traipsing across front lawns and spreading out into the streets is every imaginable character, lugging spoils from the treasure hunt called trick or treating. There is a pirate, a ghost, a gypsy, Frankenstein, a doctor, a cat, a clown, and a bride. A little girl dressed up as a bride walks along the sidewalk, her hand tucked into her father's—the shape of things to come, no doubt. At six years old, she already dreams about being a bride one day—about the one time when everyday girls get to be a princess for a day. When did little girls start dreaming about being brides? In the days when marriages were arranged and matches made out of politics and convenience, did little girls want to be brides? When did it become all she ever wanted?

For as long as I can remember I wanted to get married. Some of my earliest memories are of playing wedding and pretending to be the bride. I could turn anything into a wedding veil: a towel after a bath hung over my head and draped down my back; a pillowcase when I was supposed to be going to bed; even a T-shirt stuck to my crown as I tried to pull the too-tight opening up and over my head. I even envied my Catholic neighborhood friends because they got to wear a veil for First Communion.

I thought brides were ethereal, as if from a fairy tale. I remember peeking around the corner, spying on bridal showers hosted by my grandmother or mother. I was too young to attend but too excited to sleep at the prospect of a party, even if I wasn't invited. Who could sleep anyway with all the peals of laughter I heard while upstairs in my room? Below, the living room was filled with women showering the bride-to-be with present after present. She was always beautiful through my child eyes, dressed stylishly, a corsage on her shoulder, sitting in a seat of honor amid presents piled high—a blizzard of wrapping paper, bows, and ribbon in pastels, silver, and white. She was the center of attention, and there were more presents than Christmas and birthdays combined—what little girl wouldn't want to be a bride? And the groom? He was mysterious, whoever he was, and showed up only at the end to collect the gifts and take a little good-natured teasing from some of the other women helping in the kitchen.

As I got older it seemed the only thing that changed about me was that I got taller and I learned brides were human rather than otherworldly. My opinion about marriage was just as fantastical as it had been when I was a child. The pedestal of marriage wasn't even slightly wobbled by the fact that I'd seen the failed marriages of friends, family members, and acquaintances. My white knight, whoever he was, remained sitting firmly atop his horse.

My parents adamantly insisted I go to college, but I didn't want to—it seemed a waste of time when all I aspired to be was a wife and mother. I attended for two years then dropped out, all the while continuing to see my high school sweetheart. Finally, with the blessing of both our parents, I married my boyfriend. We'd dated seven years, and I'd planned on marrying him since we first went out. Marriage seemed the answer to my hopes, my fairy tale come true, my lifelong dream now realized. How many people could boast that?

If you were to look through our four walls and into our lives and marriage, you would see the beauty and success I'd dreamed of: three children who are loved very much, a stay-at-home mom, a husband who works hard providing for his family. Then, if you were able to see through all those things—to the heart—you would see commitment too, a commitment sustained through years of disappointment and even a betrayal.

This was a betrayal of the eyes, sight after sight that shouldn't have been seen—a discovery that awakened in the mind something that should have remained dormant. This betrayal happened a long time ago, but it's still remembered. That's the nature of betrayal, is it not? You can never completely erase it. There's a reflection of pain that remains in our eyes forever, like the spots you see after a camera flash or after looking directly at the sun.

With three children and a hearty dose of Christian guilt at the thought of divorce, my husband and I have stayed together despite this betrayal. We went to a counselor both together and separately and made the choice to keep working on our relationship.

It would be an understatement to say that this betrayal has been a crushing blow to me. But in hindsight I see how my expectations of marriage set me up for disappointment to begin with, even without the events that have transpired. No union with another fellow sinful being could ever live up to the impossible ideals I had for marriage and for my dreams.

At the beginning of every year I begin to read the Bible from Genesis on; this year, as always, I start out with enthusiasm and determination as with most New Year's resolutions, but somewhere around March I begin to lose steam—usually because I get to Leviticus and my interest wanes, unlike in Genesis and Exodus, books filled with climactic stories and drama.

Anyway, I was in the third chapter of Genesis, the one about the fall of man and the curse. To woman, God promises, "Your desire will be for your husband, and he will rule over you." Though I've read this many times over, I stopped to dwell on it, this time with a touch of resignation. I'm not a biblical scholar or even particularly knowledgeable about biblical studies, but it does seem as if a woman sexually desiring her husband isn't such a curse. Wouldn't that be a good thing?

Yet a long time ago, though I can't remember where, I was taught that the word *desire* doesn't have a sexual connotation. Rather, *desire* refers to a woman wanting to rule over her husband—her desire will be for her to be in charge, and God says no, it's better that her husband should be over her.

I can't say I really like what I've been told—I'm not completely satisfied with the explanation. Then, recently, I read an altogether different translation of the word *desire*. In her book *Woman: The Full Story*, author Michele Guinness traces the original Hebrew word *teshuqah*, which we translated as *desire*, to actually mean "turning." The curse for sin was that woman would turn toward man to fulfill her deepest desires for love and belonging rather than to God, as was intended. So therefore the second part of the sentence in Genesis 3:16, "he will rule over you," is not a mandate but a result of the turning of the woman.

This makes perfect sense to me. Think about it for a minute. We all know woman after woman who allowed a guy to treat her badly because she turned toward him rather than to God. We've probably even done this ourselves at one time or another. Our self-worth, value, and perceived happiness were all tied up in a man, so we settled, even when we knew better. By doing so, we let that man rule over us, but not in the right way—we handed him control over how we felt, what we thought of ourselves, and what we put up with. Think of the countless things done (or not done) from the time we were little girls to seduce the attention or love of a boy—in some cases a skinny, pimple-faced boy with testosterone to burn, and yet we handed him this power over us.

Doesn't this meaning of the curse make perfect sense now? It's indeed a curse. *Turning toward* is a curse for the woman because it's something she must forever fight against. This idea, this curse is important even when you marry a Christian, a good and worthy man you love and who loves you too, because he will hurt you and he'll always hurt you in little ways. Not just in big betrayals—as I experienced in my marriage—but in a million little ways like simply hurting your feelings. That's the power you give someone when you love him—a potent power that can make you feel good and bad.

When I was so deeply hurt, I felt my dreams coming down around me. And that was all I could see. The debris of my crushed ideas and illusions blinded me. I see now that I had turned—toward my dreams and my husband, whom I thought to be the fulfillment of those dreams.

I'm like the tiny ballerina that sat atop the jewelry box I had as a little girl. I would wind up the key at the back of the box and watch the ballerina turn and turn to the rhythm of some tinny-sounding music, and as the key unwound, the dancer would slow down. The music slurred and stuttered; the once graceful ballerina moved in jerky movements until she simply stopped altogether. She'd often stop facing backward so that I couldn't see her face until I turned her around.

Somewhere along the way in my marriage, I turned the wrong way, the music stopped, and I found myself facing backward rather than looking forward. I got stuck looking at a sight far less beautiful to behold, but I didn't know it. I stopped looking to God to fulfill my deepest dreams and desires. Or maybe I never learned how in the first place. And it wasn't only my eyes; maybe to avoid a crick in my neck I had turned my whole body toward something else as if to forever face backward, or at least until someone turned me.

The song, written by Helen H. Lemmel in 1922, says:

Turn your eyes upon Jesus,
Look full in His wonderful face;

141

And the things of earth will grow strangely dim
In the light of His glory and grace.

But how do you see Jesus when your vision is blurred by tears or obscured by another's reflection? How do you hold on to him when your hands are already filled with your own dreams or disappointments? How do you listen to what he's saying when the sound of your own pain pounding in your ears is all you can hear or when you can only listen to the sweet nothings whispered by someone else?

I don't know. I just keep looking and listening. I let go of what I'm holding so tightly until I can start to see again.

It's not easy, not easy at all. But when you cry and you look through your tears, everything is made bigger, almost magnified by the wetness. When the tears clear just a little, I can see a bigger picture of Jesus than I saw before, clearer and truer. He was always truer than my dreams and expectations ever were.

So that's my curse and my challenge—to keep my eyes turned toward him; not on myself, my disappointment, or my husband; not on all the millions of wonderful things my husband does for me; and not on the mistakes he's made either.

I want Jesus to come close and put his hands on either side of my face and say, "Look into my eyes. Your reflection is there." And I want him to lock eyes with me and hold my face firmly so that I can't turn my head in any other direction, no matter how the music plays on.

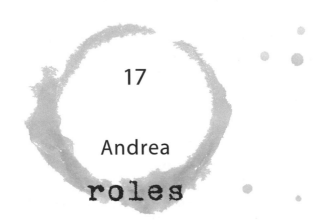

17

Andrea

roles

Marriage: a community consisting of a master, a mistress, and
two slaves—making in all two.

Ambrose Bierce

Does anyone learn how to be a sister or a daughter? What about
a friend? I mean, you just sort of become those things. Before
I was married I never gave much thought to my role as a wife
either. It just kind of seemed like something you become. And
by roles I don't just mean duties of cooking, cleaning, or mother-
ing. After all, we are far greater than the sum of the duties we
perform. There is so much more a person can do than just the
tasks we relegate to them because of their gender. To think too
narrowly, too inside the box, I am now convinced, is only to
shortchange all that we are capable of being. Even as my roles
of daughter, sister, and mother evolve and change to meet the
present needs, so does my role of wife.

143

No one told me how much the role of a wife is always changing. As a woman, I'm also a daughter, sister, and mother, but even within each of those roles I evolve and change to meet the present needs. To resist this change is to deprive one's self of all the dimensions that a woman is capable of existing in.

Of course, when I was young I didn't think too much about the spectrum of what it meant to be a wife. My notions were simple: I always wanted to get married. I never considered that I wouldn't. I had a good relationship with my father, enjoyed the company of boys, and grew up watching my parents' marriage. They loved each other, enjoyed each other's company, and had a very harmonious relationship. When I met my husband, I fell madly in love with him. Our story, were it to be summed up in a headline, would be this: Southern Beauty Queen Meets Midwest Preacher's Kid. I knew in an instant that I never wanted to be without him. I didn't think I could *live* without him.

Couples today give much more thought and care to planning for their future. I never cared about our careers, how many children we'd have, where we'd live, or what "we" would look like. I only wanted to spend the rest of our lives together. I guess my lack of thought for the future turned out to be for the best, because no sooner had we said "I do" than what few plans we had made were completely upended.

After our honeymoon, with our car packed with wedding gifts and all our belongings, we headed out to begin our new life together. We'd each lined up jobs in a city halfway across the country from where I'd been living, and my husband was going to finish his education. But before we even got started he got a call for another job.

The offer was a once-in-a-lifetime opportunity, and it seemed to fall out of the sky. So without needing too much deliberation, he took the job, and we had to tell our previous employers, whom we'd never actually worked for, that we'd not be taking those jobs after all.

This began a two-year whirlwind. We moved to a tiny town in the Midwest and into a one-bedroom apartment above the clock shop on the main street of this little town. My husband had to travel almost every weekend. So during the week we went about our usual activities, adjusting to married life and getting to know each other in our different roles, and on weekends we hit the road together.

Life was busy and simple at the same time. I thought things were good. I felt loved and was content. But then I was very compliant, which made everything less complicated.

After two years I gave birth to our first child. With a daughter to care for, I decided I wouldn't go with my husband on the weekends anymore. I got involved in a church, made some good friends, and didn't really miss all the travel. I had plenty to occupy my days.

Suddenly everything changed. Before, I'd liked being led and enjoyed following and supporting. Now it was a struggle to be independent and in charge when my husband was gone, then resume a submissive role when he returned.

A turning point came one Sunday evening when my husband came home after a weekend away and confessed many things to me, things I never wanted to hear. He was living a double life, one as dutiful and good—the husband I thought I knew—and another as though he were single and free, unaccountable to anyone, even to God. His words fell over me with a thud. I was completely blindsided, crushed; my world rocked. I felt deeply betrayed and didn't know how I ever could have the strength to show him the grace he needed.

Personally I never mustered that strength, but God enabled me to forgive things over time. Only he could do that. What was my role of companion and lover in the face of betrayal? What were my responsibilities to my husband in the face of his abandonment of his responsibility to me? I never saw my role as contingent on his role, but should it be? And if so, when did that start being the case? And God changed my husband in a miraculous way. So my husband's betrayal impacted me powerfully, but so did watching God transform my husband into the man he became—and that's the important thing about marriage. It's a union, two people so entwined that everything one spouse does affects the other, for better and for worse. Everyone says those words when they get married, but I don't think any of us have a clue what that will really mean. Not until you're tested, when the part each of you plays comes into question . . .

I think it's possible for both spouses to become better together than they ever could be apart. As my husband grew, so did I, and watching him gave me the courage to face some of my own struggles—things I'd never told anyone. As I began to share these things with him for the first time, and as we battled them together, I saw my role mutate once again. Being a wife meant that I was also a sister in Christ.

There were times when he needed me to hold him accountable or when he learned from my insight. My role is one of helpmate. I like that. I don't think it's demeaning or makes me less of a person. There's fulfillment in supporting and following.

I've learned it's also important that I'm growing in every way as a person. My husband needs me to introduce him to new insight, to be an example, and to be in a place of developing and seeking. I find it rewarding when I see my growth in him, just as his growth can be seen in me.

Some people say faith and spirituality don't affect marriage, that spirituality is between them and God. For me, faith in marriage is everything. God tells me to deny myself. No one else says that. The world says look out for yourself first. Yet marriage requires the opposite—looking out for your spouse first, to sacrifice yourself every day, to think first of your husband rather than your own wishes and desires. Marriage requires faith. Otherwise, at times such sacrifice seems like so much, too much. For me, it's a process—like all my rough edges are being sanded.

When my husband and I first started having children, it so radically altered my life that my whole reason for existence changed. Now our children have all left home. They're grown and married, and it's a new season of life for me and for us as a couple.

It's like that for everyone, ever changing in stages, in spirit, and in body.

That's the idea of change that confounds me the most in my marriage. You just never get it all figured out, no matter how many experiences you have, lessons you learn, or obstacles you overcome. Marriage is like a fire: alive, sometimes waning, other times growing, always burning, consuming, never standing still. And like a fire, marriage can't be trusted to stay the same if you turn your back on it. You can't stop nurturing, building, or feeding it for it to continue burning steadily, strongly.

My husband and I made many important decisions along the way in our marriage. We experienced failure but triumphs too. As I look back I see how critical so many of the decisions

147

that we made together were in taking us to the place we are today. At the time we knew certain decisions were significant, but I don't think we knew how irrevocably they would alter the course of our lives.

So we've come a long distance together, and it's been a wild ride for sure. I've hung on for dear life, even screamed from time to time.

And what we see as our roles in our relationship has become more fluid. It had to be that way in order to twist and turn with the ride of our lives. And I think it's better that way. Yes, we have God-given roles—I still see my husband as a leader, even when he messes up—but to see our roles too narrowly and to be stuck in them can be destructive to the relationship and will stifle the life of the union and of the two people who created it. My husband used to say that our car "turned on a dime and gave you ten cents change." I think life brings those blind turns, and you have to be able to respond and bend or you topple over.

I said in the beginning that I didn't care what my life was when I first married, that I just wanted to be with my husband. I still feel that way. I'm not quite so naive anymore, but I still don't want to live one day without my husband. We've climbed some precipitous hills. At times, it seemed like there would never be rest for our weary muscles. Then in a flash we seemed to be barreling downhill at full speed. And sometimes, just as we seemed to be rolling along in our relationship, gaining speed, another hill would be in our path. One thing's for sure: like that fire, we'll never be standing still in this journey of marriage. But then I wouldn't want to be. I can't wait to see what the next twenty-six years hold.

18

Helen

intimacy

Among intelligent people the surest basis for marriage is
friendship—the sharing of real interests—the ability to fight
out ideas together and understand each other's thoughts and
dreams.

Khalil Gibran

What is it that people really want from God? For the last few
weeks I have turned this question over in my mind. What we
truly seek from God, I believe, is something we inherently
seek. So then that begs the question: what are we created for
that we seek to find in people around us? What is at the root
of our longing in relationship?

I guess I can only speak for myself, but if I were to delve
deep into the depths of my soul, I think the answer would
be acceptance. What greater thing than to be known and accepted? To be loved not only in spite of who you are but

because of who you are. That is what I think we want from God and from our most intimate relationships, beginning with the approval we seek from a parent and then moving to the same approval we seek from a spouse. But what is the price we are willing to pay to be known so fully? Can something so precious be easy to find? And if you find it, is there a cost or a quid pro quo?

As a young woman, I never thought I'd get married, and I absolutely didn't think I'd have children (I now have four). I was strong, career driven, and independent, and I wasn't looking for a man who would tell me what to do. In fact, that was what I feared happened in marriage.

Nevertheless, by the time I was twenty-six, I'd dated a lot of guys. *Maybe I'll get married,* I decided, *but only to someone who's exactly what I want in a man.* I was afraid that I would have to give up my dreams, that my potential would be wasted, and that I would lose control over my life. I think as I matured I became more sure of myself. I had more confidence that I could continue my dreams and that I wouldn't lose myself to marriage, but rather that both could exist harmoniously together. Still, I wasn't desperate to find someone.

I wasn't going to settle for anything—anyone—less. So I ended a two-year relationship with a man I'd thought was ideal when we first started dating—a man I thought possessed everything I wanted: he was tall (he had to be taller than me, of course), good looking, financially secure, and a Christian. In spite of the fact that he hit all the high points on my Ideal Husband List, there was something lacking—a connecting of souls. I came to realize this stemmed from a depth of faith that he didn't have. To him, Christianity was about rules and a list of don'ts.

I had wrestled with that already and had moved on.

I'd been raised in a traditional Southern Baptist home and went through a period of rebellion in college, where I exercised my hurt and anger toward my parents, men, and legalism. I did what I wanted just because I could—and I'd since realized that all my acting out was against God more than anyone else; it was God I was hurting most. Once I was in that place of conviction, renewal, and grace, I saw my faith as much more than laws and guidelines to live by. I saw the dos and the whys, not just the don'ts.

I knew I had a personal relationship with God that I wanted to continue to grow for the rest of my life. So, my long list of all that I thought I wanted in a man became reduced to really just one thing: a man who loved the Lord and wanted to grapple with faith and life the way I did.

The thing is, I'm a wrestler. The way I see it, there are basically two kinds of Christians. There are those who just live with their faith, not really questioning or testing but instead believing with simplicity and childlikeness. Then there are those of us who wrestle, testing and questioning before believing (and even in the midst of believing). Wrestlers are the ones who come to faith not quite as neatly as the others.

I decided I needed a partner who would wrestle with me and really understand that part of who I am.

And so that's when I met him at a party. After our first date, I knew: I could spend the rest of my life with this man.

I didn't have the unrealistic expectations for my marriage that many women seem to have. I've always attributed this to the fact that when we got married I was a little bit older and well informed. I didn't think our life was going to be a happily-ever-after fairy tale of bliss; I knew we wouldn't always have sappy, romantic feelings for one another.

But I did enter marriage with the expectation that our marriage would meet my desires. (Why else would you get married, really?) It never entered my mind that my husband might have different desires than I did or that our desires just might challenge one another's.

In truth, the person I saw myself to be in the light of marriage took me aback. I began seeing flaws I never knew existed. It was like seeing one of those pictures in a beauty magazine of someone's face under an ultraviolet light: a seemingly beautiful woman by all external appearances is reduced to hideous under the ultraviolet rays. You see all the sun damage and age marks on her skin. You're horrified and vow never again to go in the sun. Of course, resolutions like that last about as long as the rest of the winter and early spring; by the first warm day, you've forgotten.

In marriage, such harshness isn't easily forgotten. My selfishness stared at me head-on every day. That's what it was too: seemingly innocent expectations to have my desires met translated quickly to selfishness and demanding-ness. I realized fast that I truly didn't know how to give of myself in the way that marriage required. For example, I expected my husband to support my career and give himself to the advancement of it, but I didn't do the same for him. I was insistent about the time I wanted him to give to me and to our children after they were born, yet I didn't look for ways to lighten his burden so that he could do just that.

Given my level of achieved maturity and personal success, this was deplorable to me. I had spent so much of my life trying to get it right. How had I missed something this big? I told myself I needed to learn how to give up my own desires. I needed to learn what being a partner and helpmate meant—clichés I wanted to believe in but that carried no practical meaning in my everyday life. I was going to have to inject meaning into those words if they were ever to inhabit my life with my husband.

But during this time my husband and I had two children, and I began to feel that more and more I was losing ownership of my body. If it wasn't breastfeeding or having a child cuddling with me or a dog or cat crawling over me, then it was my husband needing that physical connection.

As soon as we were married—beginning on our honeymoon, really—it became very apparent that I couldn't keep up with him sexually. That man has the stamina of a prize-winning racehorse. I probably enjoyed sex more than many of my friends, but can you please tell me what woman can do it every day, twice a day? He didn't understand how I couldn't keep up with him, and so fight after intense fight ensued over the same subject.

When I'd say no or beg off due to fatigue or illness, I'd feel terribly guilty. I'd gently tell him, "Not tonight, honey," with promises of the next night and assurances of my attraction to him. I'd turn over in the bed and lie there in the dark feeling like a failure as a wife. Then I'd wake the next day feeling the same dread as I moved about my morning routine . . . until our eyes would meet and I could see for myself that my husband still loved me. It wasn't only because we fought about it, but I suppose those feelings also came from my own perceptions about the role of a wife.

The culmination of all these feelings meant that I wanted to take my body back once and for all. I wanted to bite back at anyone who attempted to touch me! Only I didn't know how to tell my husband how I felt about all of this.

I began to think that even though we were fighting, we weren't actually communicating. Even when we weren't fighting and had great discussions on the weekends or sometimes in the evening when we were home together, I was afraid to tell him what I really thought. I never opened the depth of my soul, my feelings and my angst, fearing that it would be like the opening of Pandora's box.

Thank goodness I finally realized that we had to delve into those depths if we were ever going to get anywhere. I saw that giving my body to him in lovemaking was an act of surrender, a giving of my whole self. But for men it's not that way. A husband totally surrenders when he gives his emotional self, not just his body. I needed that emotional surrender from him—to know his deepest thoughts and feelings if I was going to surrender my body. And I told him this.

Finally, we began to talk. We started out safe, and slowly, eventually, over a period of many conversations, we talked about sex, our pasts, our feelings and impressions, and our fears. I've since told my husband things I could never tell another soul; he's the keeper of my deepest thoughts and my darkest past. He's since shared in equal depth with me.

And over the years of our marriage, that depth was practiced time and time again. And I saw the kind of man my husband really was. As I struggled with immense disappointment, loss, and betrayals in relationships, hurts that happened outside my marriage but that often manifested into bitterness on my part within my marriage, what I saw from my husband was support and patience. He allowed me to grieve in my own way. I felt things he never would have felt, and I had thoughts he did not understand, and yet he waited patiently for me to work through my emotions. And he never forced it in his time. He simply waited, just like Jesus does for us. He waits and he waits until we come to the place he wants us to be.

In truth, my marriage has taught me not only about who I am but also about who I can become. It's not just the tidal waves and undertow, the powers and struggles beyond my control, that have taught me about my reality and my possibilities. It's been the beauty and serenity of my partner, the man I married seventeen years ago. He's truly loved me the way Christ loves the church. He's given himself up for me over and over again, in a million ways, some great, many small.

I think back to a time when we were first married. Settled in bed, I was warm under a mound of covers, and it was cold outside. We lay side by side, each reading our own book, when I remarked that I was thirsty but didn't want to get up and get some water. Without a word my husband put down his book and padded to the kitchen to fetch a drink for me. I lay there in bed, humbled. *Would I have done that for him?*

I didn't always push my comforts aside to meet his needs the way he did mine.

Marriage is incredibly hard work. Isn't that what we all say? What I mean is, it's truly relentless.

I think it would be easier in many ways for me to be single. But no matter the work, I've never doubted that it's worth every minute. It's through this man that I've been shown a picture of Christ, and it's caused me to draw closer to him. It's only through my marriage that I've seen myself, and that I've changed and learned. It's only through my marriage that I've been championed and cheered on. Through this I've learned the meaning of the words *partner* and *helpmate*. They mean being an encourager, meeting the needs of each other, loving, supporting with true strength, and respecting each other.

It's only through this marriage that I've experienced the greatest testing but the truest reward. Only through this marriage have I discovered such beauty and treasure—beauty that I was created for.

Our children like to hear us tell a story over and over about how we almost killed each other when we first started dating. I'd gotten into scuba diving and decided to take lessons. My husband volunteered to take the lessons with me so that we could learn and enjoy the activity together. One day, we were given a buddy-breathing exercise. Relegated into teams of two, we were to go down to the depths with our partner and then take turns breathing from the same tank.

Because my husband, like most men, is ever the competitor, he was determined to beat the other teams in the class. He insisted that we both work to that end. We could have killed each other by not breathing when we were supposed to and rushing the exercise.

But scuba diving reminds me of the journey of intimacy. We now move and live with a connection so deep, as deep as the sea. It's in the deep that treasure can be found—a knowing of each other that comes only from descending the depths together. Down and down we go until our toes touch the sand at the bottom of the sea of our souls. Here is where we learn how to breathe together; here, I have no desire ever to come back up. Having tasted of the deep, the surface life is no longer for me.

We have been married for seventeen years, and I say talk to me in another seventeen and we'll still be swimming around down here. Our skin may be wrinkled (especially if we stay in the water all that time), but I think I would like to grow some fins and scales and never emerge from the beauty of this sea world again.

19

Shannon

expectations

> There isn't a wife in the world who has not taken the exact measure of her husband, weighed him and settled him in her own mind, and knows him as well as if she had ordered him after designs and specifications of her own.
>
> Charles Dudley Warner

As long as I live I'll never forget waking up during our first night together. We'd both been asleep after an awkward honeymoon night, which I guess is fairly normal for two virgins as ignorant as we were about sex. I was a little shell-shocked, but I snuggled up beside him, my body tucked into the curve of his large frame. I remember thinking how he was so big and I was so small, yet my body fit perfectly into his. I paid attention to him breathing deeply and rhythmically beside me.

In that moment, it was our souls—our spirits and emotions—that seemed to perfectly fit together, like spoons or two pieces of a puzzle.

Everything was just right in my world. I felt so safe, so secure. I knew I was created for this, to be with this man. I belonged to him and he to me. This was the most intensely satisfying feeling I'd known.

Who knew times would follow when our ideas and emotions would not fit together at all—years when rather than intense satisfaction I'd feel extreme frustration and disappointment?

Sometimes even our bodies seemed to grow apart.

One of my first disappointments was that I wanted sex more frequently than my husband. He would go two or three weeks and not want to be together, and I didn't feel that I could say anything to him about this. I was afraid of conflict, but this situation hurt me deeply. I felt rejected and was sure there must be something wrong with me. How could I not feel those things? All I knew was that I desired him, and he only seemed to feel the same every couple of weeks.

Looking for answers, I even attended a women's seminar on relationships. Afterward I shared with the instructor my struggle. She was sympathetic but said she'd never really heard of that. The issue of frequency of sex usually originated from the woman not desiring sex as often as her husband, not the other way around. All my friends complained about how often their husbands wanted sex, often rolling their eyes and shaking their heads whenever the subject came up. I usually remained quiet, too ashamed to share with them what my situation was.

I began to look at myself. *What am I expecting in marriage?*

I don't think there was ever a time when I didn't want to get married or have a husband and family of my own. I grew up a pastor's daughter in a strict disciplinarian home where there were high expectations for behavior and achievement, and my father set the bar for everything. He didn't want my brother and me to express negative emotions. Though my parents expressed anger to us, we were never permitted to respond in kind, so feelings of frustration and sadness churned inside me. I never really knew how to deal properly with those emotions. I also yearned for acceptance and feared I'd never measure up.

In spite of this authoritarian culture, I knew I was loved, without doubt.

I also had a rich spiritual heritage planted in me. Our father loved to teach, and we loved to learn by listening and watching him. We all hold knowledge so dear. I remember long road trips when it seemed we would never reach our destination, yet we passed the time by learning. My father would tell me to dig into his briefcase and fish out his pack of memory verses—a wad of memory cards tied together with a bulging rubber band. He would recite them from memory as, verse by verse, I followed every word on the cards, carefully correcting any misspoken words.

He asked me questions about the verses he was memorizing: what did that mean? How might it apply to my life right then in elementary school or when I played with my friends?

So I grew up seeing a husband as the spiritual leader of the family. Those expectations were fed later too, during the time I dated my husband.

When we first met (at my father's church), he was dating one of my friends. After a date she would call me and report how the evening had gone: he was always the perfect gentleman and spiritual leader, not to mention good looking! I longed to date someone like him. So when he and my friend broke up, parting on good terms, she suggested he and I spend some time together.

On our first date we talked well into the middle of the night. We shared even on that first night our hopes, desires, and concerns for our individual futures. Then as we dated, often he'd read the Bible to me and we'd discuss it. We had such a meeting of the minds and understood so much about one another in such a short time that I felt as though we'd been friends half of our lives.

When we eventually married I had many expectations for what our lives together would be like, but I never knew exactly what those expectations were, or even that I had them, until they weren't met. Isn't that the way of expectations? We never think to voice them and talk them over beforehand, but when they aren't met it seems as if all heaven and earth hang on them.

So now here I was in a marriage where my expectations weren't met. The main problem was our sexual expectations— and I'd already wondered if the problem was me. But I'd only contemplated my physical appearance and sexual prowess, not my attitude. So as disappointment built upon disappointment, I began to feel bitter toward my husband—and I was unable to deal with negative emotions. I buried my hurt and frustration, and they began to seep like a slow leak, showing up in my attitude, my words, and actions.

I became a nag.

I nagged my husband about how he spoiled our children (I felt like the bad person all the time—always the disciplinarian), how he spent money, and—worst—how he lacked spiritual leadership.

The latter was such a profound disappointment to me. He'd been so spiritually minded before we were married; this was one of the things I'd sought out in a mate and what had attracted me to him. Now all those characteristics seemed to have vanished. He never wanted to have family devotions with our children. I had to drag him to church most Sundays. Night after night before bed I'd read my Bible while he dozed off to sleep, his Bible literally collecting dust on his nightstand.

So I hassled him some more, not knowing how to handle my exasperation or go about getting my way.

One day I was home by myself, and in the solitude my frustrations boiled inside me. I decided I was going to pack up every Bible in the house as my way of saying to my husband, "Fine, if you're not going to make an effort, we'll just be a pagan family. We won't be Christians anymore." So I went around the house and gathered every single Bible I could find: King James versions, NIVs, little pocket New Testaments, study Bibles, and the children's picture Bibles. I packed them into a box and tossed a couple of concordances in there too, then taped it shut.

Seeming to have gained physical strength from my anger, I heaved the box up into the attic, where it sat, unnoticed, for three days.

The following Sunday morning, as we were getting ready to leave for church, I heard my husband muttering to himself, "Where have all the Bibles in the house gone?" I kept quiet. All day long. Until that night as we were getting into bed. Suddenly my Bible tantrum struck me as funny. I began laughing, and asked if he really wanted to know where the Bibles were.

I don't think he was going to lose any sleep over it, but he asked, "Yeah, where?" I told him of my temper fit and the Bible raid that had occurred earlier that week. We chuckled together over my foolishness, except it really wasn't that funny to me. Inside, I was crushed. I cried out to God. How could asking for my husband to be a spiritual leader not be in God's will? It was a righteous desire!

I didn't understand why God wouldn't change the situation. Then one night I watched a documentary on the life of singer Keith Green. I knew some of Keith's music, the more well-known songs like "There Is a Redeemer" and "Oh Lord, You're Beautiful" and how they continue to impact people. And I knew he'd died in a tragic plane crash in 1982, but I didn't really know his story.

When Keith, once a searching skeptic and hippie in the '70s, first became a Christian, he'd already been a musician for some time. In his teenage years he was pegged as the Next Big Thing; the music industry knew Keith was a talent. He packed out and filled up the California hotspots whenever he played. His same passion for music now blazed for Christ and for those lost and searching.

Keith wanted to minister to the lost through music that glorified God; he never desired to make "Christian music." Christians already had plenty of great music, and they already had the truth too, Keith reasoned. So he was driven to make secular albums that showed Jesus and reached people in pain and doubt.

It sounded like a great plan—the Great Commission, after all—and there was no doubt God had blessed Keith with the talent to carry that out. He auditioned for record company after record company, vying for a contract that most in the industry thought was rightfully his anyway. Yet every time he was turned down. Rejected. Door after door closed in his face. Inexplicably, there was great interest in him, yet he couldn't get signed by a secular record company.

Why wouldn't God want to use this California hippie to bring others to himself?

Keith was forced to reevaluate the path he thought God had for him. He realized God was leading him to Christian music after all. He followed God's leading, signed a recording contract with Sparrow Records, and never looked back.

There's no denying the power and reach of Keith Green's ministry, even years after his passing; what occurred to me in watching his story unfold, already knowing the ending, was that even something that seems so right and even godly is not always God's will or best plan for us. Sometimes God really does shut the doors of good intentions and noble desires for something different, something better.

I thought of my own life. Suddenly I was trying to see myself through my husband's eyes, trying to feel what he must feel. I realized I wasn't someone I would enjoy coming home to. Whether that was the reason for infrequent lovemaking or not, I knew I'd become bitter and unlikable.

Right then, right there in that moment, I earnestly sought God, praying and reading and asking him to change my heart.

But God worked on my sight first. He opened my eyes to the many wonderful things my husband was doing for me, how supportive he was of me in a million little ways: taking out the trash, helping around the house, always filling my car with gas. Those were the things I'd always heard other wives complain about, and here my husband was actually taking care of all these things for me. Then I thought of the big things: my husband loved me with an acceptance I'd never known. He always told me that I exceeded his expectations, and he never picked at me or was critical toward me, even though I often criticized him.

Something in me shifted then. It wasn't as if the things that had been bothering me suddenly didn't matter anymore, or that I began to live in denial. Rather, I chose to turn my eyes toward the many wonderful things about my husband.

Years later, with the inevitable wisdom of hindsight, I glimpsed what perhaps was God's plan in all of this. I was raised with a very spiritual father, who taught me relentlessly and taught me well about spirituality—how to grow as a believer. Could it be that God knew I didn't need someone else to be responsible for my spiritual growth? Could it be that I'd already been given the tools to pursue a deeper spirituality on my own, just God and me?

What was marriage giving me then?

There was no doubt that what I found in my husband was acceptance—complete and unconditional. I didn't really know my own needs, no matter how much I thought I did—but God did.

I wish I could say that after I got all that figured out, our marriage was simple and easy. But of course you would know that isn't true. It's never easy. Our divide wasn't only created by unreasonable expectations. We still had a long road to go in learning to be able to talk about our feelings, our hurts, learning to fight and disagree constructively. And I had to learn how to be real.

A firstborn perfectionist, raised by another perfectionist, I was terribly afraid of failing and messing up. I thought if I didn't show weakness or sin, others would think I didn't have any. I knew of grace, but I was also very consumed by the law and always doing the right thing. I knew I was supposed to be like Christ, but I lived that principle as if I were supposed to measure up to him, and, obviously, I never could.

A turning point came when I decided to volunteer with a women's group in our community, a service for hurting women struggling with addictions, depression, eating disorders, and the like. During the first evening meeting I attended, a woman stood up and with transparent honesty spoke of her relationship with her father and the pain in her life as a result. I was shaken and shocked by her blatant frankness. *Surely she was wrong to share so much, so openly,* I thought.

The next week it was the same. A different woman confessing her hurts but with the same kind of raw openness. Again I resisted such openness and wondered about the good of this kind of airing of one's most intimate concerns. But week after week I went back, honoring my commitment to try to minister to these women, and little by little I learned from them.

Rather than me helping them as I'd smugly intended, they helped me by opening my eyes to a realness I'd never before encountered. I saw raw honesty shared in an appropriate environment and how it could catapult one to growth and change.

I looked over my life and realized I'd never been able to tell my parents what I really felt. I'd never been able to tell my husband in a productive manner when my feelings were hurt—when I was angry or disappointed. I'd never been able to share with my friends the struggles I dealt with, always sure they would never understand and afraid they would think less of me.

So I went home after one of these meetings and told my husband that I wanted to be more real and honest with him—but that it was going to be ugly. I knew that being real wasn't always pretty. I explained to him that I wanted to do this because I thought in the end it would draw us together. He agreed, and probably braced himself for the onslaught that was sure to follow. But my taking the initiative to bring our relationship to a more honest and intimate level opened the door for him to do the same, and the funny thing is, we started communicating in a way we never had before. We actually acknowledged present issues. For one thing, we fought in a way we never had before. But we came to a resolution—something we hadn't done before. I realize now that fighting, if done gainfully, is useful and healthy.

I also realized that I put unreasonable expectations not only on my husband but also on myself as well. Crossing a threshold where I was able to be real with myself caused those expectations to crumble, and I was able to see eye to eye with a man who I was really looking at honestly for the first time. I forgot all about my expectations, and they were replaced by honest intimacy.

Over time we learned to embrace our feelings rather than push them away. And I grew not only in my relationship with my husband but also with God. Being honest with my husband somehow enabled me to come before God with more honesty—and my view changed. For the first time I was able to sense God's delight in me as his child, and I stopped focusing so much on measuring up and getting depressed over what I saw in myself. I learned that God could use me in spite of my failings; that great as my sin often seems, God is greater.

Now, when I look back over the years we've been together I see how we are truly greater together than we are apart. Like the saying "the whole is greater than the sum of its parts." Not that our relationship is perfect by any means. We're still two imperfect and very different individuals, but we think so much as one, completing each other's sentences, knowing what the other is thinking. That two people can work through so many disagreements and do it over and over again, staying together all through their lives, is just the mystique of God's working; it never stops amazing me that two people so totally different can be molded into one.

Sometimes I wonder why God designed marriage that way. Just the gender differences alone can be baffling and even seemingly insurmountable. Yet here we are. What I at first saw as a lack of action on the part of God, I now see as his deep love and involvement with my future because he didn't change my circumstances. He changed me, revealed to me who I really am. It took decades, and I sure wouldn't want to go back and do it all over again. But I see now, I understand.

Even the bad had a purpose.

20

Julia

the sacredness
of marriage

When people get married because they think it's a long-time love affair, they'll be divorced very soon because all love affairs end in disappointment. But marriage is a recognition of a spiritual identity.

Joseph Campbell

I look into the full-length mirror to take in every inch of meticulously chosen bridal attire. With an impeccably manicured hand, I smooth an imaginary wrinkle in the skirt of my white satin dress. *There.* I couldn't be more pleased with the result. I feel like a princess. But today is no fairy tale, no fantasy. Indeed, today is fantastically real. The path I traveled to get here is so very real too . . . only today that journey seems a million miles away.

You see, I'm standing on the threshold of my second marriage. In a few moments my feet will take those monumental steps down the aisle of this little chapel. I'm fortified by my knowledge of the past, though this is a place I haven't been before, and I'm only a shadow of who I used to be.

What I mean is that to say "this time will be different" seems cliché, yet I know in my heart it's rightfully true.

What makes it so? What have I discovered, what do I know, and what do I now believe that assures me this union will be unlike anything I previously knew?

I grew up like so many others in a devout Christian home—I was always held to a very high standard. As the adventurous, passionate, middle child, I always seemed like I was on a fast track. I pushed myself ahead in almost every dimension of my life—with education, coming-of-age privileges, rules—and in my own way. Maybe I was trying to blaze a unique path, stand out, or settle some restlessness within myself. Whatever the reason, and like I was with every other landmark growing up, I couldn't wait to get married.

In my teen years, I yo-yoed between a few less than spectacular boyfriends. By my early twenties I settled on a person who seemed the antithesis of all the others. He seemed mature and responsible. He had goals and aspirations. Looking back, I see plenty of reasons for some doubts and hesitations. But would it have mattered then? I'd probably have thought, *I've come too far to turn back now.* Besides, any doubt would have demanded action—action I wasn't secure enough in myself to take, though I didn't know that yet.

So, less than twenty-four hours after committing to this man for the rest of my life, I knew I'd made a terrible mistake.

I discovered things I never could have known beforehand. Anyway, the naiveté with which I made the decision to marry was irreversibly shattered. Instantly, I became wise beyond my years, but it was a heartbreaking wisdom. But I felt it was too late to be able to apply that wisdom.

Feeling I had no other choice, silently, I resigned myself to my new life and forged dutifully ahead as the committed wife and Christian. I couldn't possibly tell my parents and family—their disappointment would devastate me. Besides, liberation wouldn't be an option. In fact, it was eternally prohibited. I was a Christian, and divorce was not only frowned upon, it was criminal.

As time went by, my circumstances worsened, and my acquired knowledge of the man I lived with made life unbearable. When I saw how he began to treat me, what went on in his private life, and the things he really cared about, I imagined myself in a ghastly prison with only a one-sided window. I could look out and see the green pastures of freedom, but no one could see inside to the conditions I was forced to endure.

Even though mine was a faith that at its cornerstone was based on grace, forgiveness, and second chances, I had no second chances. What did I know about what to do with the rest of my life? How could I predict the life I would want at forty-five? How can a twenty-three-year-old girl possibly know what she would want at thirty, at forty, at fifty? And yet . . . girls make those choices every day.

I'd chosen and chosen badly. I thought back to girls in college who were married and still unable to decide on a major. They couldn't even pick a course of study, but they had chosen a human being with whom to spend the rest of their time on earth—and the younger they married, the longer they'd be married, most likely. I read some time ago that if you couldn't pick a china pattern, you couldn't pick a spouse. Interesting theory. Perhaps there's truth to it.

I heard myself saying, *So this is it? This is the end? I am irrevocably sentenced with no chance of parole?* It didn't add up to me. I began to explore the idea of divorce and how it fit with me.

You know when you're thinking about buying a certain car, and all of a sudden it seems like every third person on the road is driving it? That's how it seemed when my thoughts began to drift to the possibility of divorce. It seemed like people were talking about divorce more than ever, and usually negatively. Divorce was derogatory, the scarlet *D*, it seemed. So I listened to the talk and weighed it with what I was taught—and I began to question all of it.

It was the questions that led me to discover the profound truths about marriage that I'd taken for granted or maybe never really understood. *Why is divorce singled out as so great a sin? What does it mean when God says he hates divorce? Why do we as Christians heap so much judgment on someone already experiencing such immense pain and disappointment?* It doesn't matter what others think of the choices I made or even the ideas I questioned. Ultimately I stand before God, and what I learned about marriage is for all of us who are married or want to be married, if we really believe what we say we do.

My husband never thought for a second that I would consider divorce; until the bitter end he never believed I'd go through with it. But one night after we arrived home from a counseling session I raised the subject. He thought I was bluffing. *Why?* I wondered. *Why doesn't he believe me? Does he think he can do whatever he wants and I am bound to stay? Does he take my wedding vow commitment to mean there are no penalties for his actions, no commitments on his part? Isn't it, after all, human nature to push as far as you can to take advantage until someone stops you and levies the consequences?*

It was for him. One night in a heated argument he actually said, "I may not love, honor, and cherish you, but I will do this until death do us part!"

I couldn't believe what I'd heard. Did he think our marriage vows were a cafeteria plan or an a la carte menu where he could just pick and choose what he wanted and discard the rest? It was as if he'd said, "Yes, I'd like the Till Death Do Us Part Special, please, but hold the Love and Honor, and can you put the Cherish on the side?"

My immediate reaction was thoughts like this: *Is he kidding? Yes, please sign me up for that one. A death sentence, to be sure!* Then I thought about it. His words, his intent were so extreme, so horrible, but were they so uncommon? Hadn't he just put into words what so many of us actually do in our marriages—and when put this way, was this kind of relationship at all palatable?

How many times had I heard a raging sermon about the evils of divorce, but how many had I heard on cherishing, valuing, showing infinite love or care in marriage? I'd heard plenty of gossip about Mr. and Mrs. X getting divorced, but not much was said about Mr. X not honoring Mrs. X, not treating her with great respect and admiration when he put her down in public or never helped her with the kids. I never heard how scandalous that was.

I was bowled over by my discovery. I was sure I deserved to be on *Oprah* for this one. We say our vows before God, and as Christians we say we can't break those vows, and therefore divorce is wrong. But what about all the promises that precede the final one—"until death do us part"? Why have those fallen by the wayside? When did God say that was the only part of the vows that mattered, or that the other vows were less important? No one would actually say this is true, but we live as if it is, don't we? If we treat our vows that way, it's only legalism, a contract, not a commitment, and not at all what I believe God has in mind for marriage.

Okay, so I uncovered what I considered to be a glaring inconsistency. So what then? What is marriage supposed to be, what do the vows really mean?

Now, we all know the Sunday school answer is that marriage was created to be an example of how Christ loved us, his church. But do we even know, I mean really know, what that means?

To me, that means marriage is a gift, some would even say a sacrament, an earthly symbol of God's immense, immeasurable love for us. To be living examples of that is no small attempt. God, in his love for us, only looks to what's best for us, never his own needs. He never cuts us down, never competes with us, never treats us disrespectfully, never shuts us out. He always treats us with kindness, compassion, fairness, openness, and grace. Marriage was created by God for two people made in God's image, joined together as a symbol of his love for us. That means it's sacred—sacred like communion is sacred.

But some of us use marriage because we want to have sex, or we've already had sex and we feel guilty, or we're lonely, or we think getting married is easier than breaking up, or we're looking for fulfillment, or we want to have the event of a wedding, or we want to be grown up and independent and marriage is a vehicle to achieve independence.

Sure, marriage should and does fill some of those many needs. But too many of us forget about the sacredness.

I know my husband and I did. And I still wonder how things could have been different if we'd had such a high esteem for marriage that we held fast to a sacred view. Would we have chosen to marry for different reasons? Would we have chosen different people to spend the rest of our lives with? Would we be different after we were married, both in how we treated one another and how we allowed ourselves to be treated? Would issues like respect, compassion, sacrifice, intimacy, and selflessness look totally different—not only in how we behaved but in how we permitted ourselves to be treated as children of God?

How might marriage, in turn, be a beautiful symbol of the love of God if its sacredness were revered?

I've thought about these things a long while, and I've let those words *the love of God*—the concept of it—spill over me in a new way. I've searched for the meaning beyond religious verbiage or clichés. I see how I've heard this certain phrase so often that for a time I forgot what it really meant.

I would never try to tell anyone whether divorce is the right or wrong choice—my point isn't to charge down that path. Stay with me . . . because I'm not really talking about divorce at all. I'm talking about marriage; you don't have to leave one to discover the same things I did about it. And here it is: for me, leaving a marriage was about examining what I really believed about my faith, about what God intended for me then and now, about forgiveness and grace, and about marriage as God designed it, and the truth of what that means.

175

So here I am. In the bridal room with a few moments of solitude before this ceremony and the next stage of my life. My heart flutters with excitement and anticipation, but I'm realistic enough to know that what I came to know, what I've described, is a tall order. I'm not foolish enough to think I'll ever live the sacredness of marriage anywhere near perfectly. But I've had a change of philosophy, a change of the lenses that I look through. I've changed from my fashionable, trendy eyeglasses to something more serious and studious. Maybe I look a little nerdy to some folks, not as much frivolous fun, but marriage is that serious. God intended it to be solemn. Sure, a husband and wife can be romantic and playful toward each other, fun at times—a lot of times. But commitment that lasts a lifetime and really "doing marriage right" is sobering. You not only have to see marriage through the eyes of God, but you have to see your mate, and yourself. Everything should look different; you should feel that difference. If you're not weighed down by the gravity of your vows, then you're not ready to take them.

The Miracle of Marriage

conclusions

Marriage is an Athenic weaving together of families, of two souls with their individual fates and destinies, of time and eternity—everyday life married to the timeless mysteries of the soul.

Thomas Moore

One of the wise and insightful women I interviewed for this book remarked that men have only five needs. Yes, only five.

Lots of sex.

A supportive wife.

A tidy home.

Good food.

Well-behaved children.

While I can't authoritatively speak to generalizations made about men, I think we'd all agree that women are not quite so simple. We're fantastically complex. Mysterious.

I've heard it said that since both man and woman were created in the image of God, each manifest different characteristics of God, the feminine and the masculine. I believe that one of the characteristics of God manifested in women is mystery—glorious and profound mystery. A man could live nearly his whole life with the same woman, and she could still confound and surprise him. And though men often lament this fact, I really think they wouldn't want it any other way. After all, only having five needs seems a little lackluster to me . . . but maybe that's just because I am a woman.

Though the mysteriousness of woman is a universally known fact, it hasn't stopped many folks from trying to place us in a category to better get their arms around our gender.

"Women want security," it's said.

True. Many women want security. But I've always resisted great sweeping characterizations made about women—or anyone, for that matter; you can't put groups of people in a single box, especially half of all humans.

One woman told me that if you had a husband who was faithful, solid, and stable, and let you stay home with your kids . . . well, then you had won the life lottery.

That idea of the life lottery intrigued me, and I began asking other women when I was interviewing them what the life lottery was to them. Their answers, incredibly diverse, surprised me.

While security was the life lottery for one, it was not so for another; for a third, it was companionship. This makes me think we should embrace our mystery and our uniqueness as being from God, a reflection of him in us. We're fantastically unique and can learn from each other in our diversity.

We can also learn from what we share in common; each story in this book held its own defeats and triumphs. I think this is because often the ability to learn and to grow involves embracing not only the lovely and pleasant but also what's messy and dark. I pray that you've gained wisdom for your own labor from the circumstances of these stories. These women bravely opened up their lives to us and revealed some poignant emotions, some profound questions, and some difficult experiences.

Most of what I've learned has been in the valleys. Strange, how the darker times can be the most illuminating and revealing. Amazing, how when you're in a place so dark that you can't see your hand in front of your face, that there you see with abundance, making the most startling revelations about life, faith, and self. The disclosures in the dark are the ones we never forget. It's through some of our bitterest times that we learn about God, his relationship to us, and his character.

Almost without exception, the women I interviewed for this project, no matter how long the duration of marriage, said marriage was like a mirror. We all see our reflections, temporarily distorted or not, through marriage—whether that mirror is like the distorted reflections we see at a carnival in a House of Mirrors, or the one in which Snow White's evil queen beholds herself as the fairest of all (only to finally see that was not the case), or the watery one in which the ugly duckling saw it had turned into a beautiful and graceful swan. We see more than only a two-dimensional image staring back at us. We see the history, sinfulness, woundedness, soulfulness; in the end, we see strength and we see grace.

The Horse Whisperer by Nicholas Evans is such a story of brokenness and healing. It centers on a young girl who is in a terrible collision while she and her best friend are riding their horses early one snowy morning. The crash is critical, and twelve-year-old Grace survives the accident amid immense loss that includes the death of her best friend, the am-

179

putation of her leg, the loss of normalcy and innocence of adolescence, and the ruin of unflinching trust between a girl and her horse.

The horse, Pilgrim, manages to survive as well, but in addition to ghastly wounds he is emotionally traumatized.

Unwilling to put the horse down and unable to reach through the pain to her daughter, the girl's mother, Annie, in utter desperation and strength of will, packs up her obstinate daughter and her frenetic horse and drives them west toward Montana to enlist the expertise of a horse whisperer—a horse whisperer who has already positively declared to Annie he will not help her.

So begins the healing of this embittered girl and her mother, the horse, and even Tom, the whisperer.

After many months and much progress for all involved, there is growth, forgiveness, and renewed hope. Finally, it is time for Grace to ride Pilgrim again. Tom has worked tirelessly with the horse to bring him to a place of emotional and physical restoration. He's made more progress than any expert thought possible. But this is the biggest test of all. Onlookers watch in hushed trepidation and hope as Grace timidly approaches Pilgrim in the corral. He acknowledges her as she steps into the ring. He still knows her—her voice and touch echo of the understanding they used to share. And yet . . .

Before she is even able to place her good leg in the stirrup and lift herself on top of him, the horse begins to buck. Sensing her fear, Pilgrim rears up whenever she steps toward him. Tears of fear and failure spring to Grace's eyes.

Tom immediately takes charge and gets hold of the horse. He tells Grace that he is going to have to do something with

Pilgrim that he hoped he wouldn't have to, and so he gives her the option to leave rather than watch.

She insists on staying.

Aided by another wrangler, Tom picks up a rope and ties it to the saddle horn, then slips a rope halter over the horse in place of the bridle. He then makes a loop with the other end of the rope, circling it around one of Pilgrim's front legs. The horse, aware of Tom moving around him, does nothing until Tom tightens the loop and forces his front leg to be lifted off the ground, consequently crippling him. This magnificent animal is now three-legged, and in fear he fights to free his leg. Tom works intently with gentle determination, trying to block out the tearful faces of Annie and Grace as they watch in horror, not understanding how Tom could be so cruel. Tom begins to tighten the lines of rope on the horse in an effort to force him down to the ground. And that tragic horse, still bearing scars of healed wounds, both inside and out, even now finds the strength to resist Tom as he fights to stay standing.

Finally in defeat, Pilgrim lays down, still and sweaty. But it's not over.

Tom calls over a sobbing Grace. As she approaches he asks her to sit beside Pilgrim and gently rub him—his head, his neck, his limbs, his belly. Lovingly, she moves her hands over the once gloriously beautiful horse, and the horse follows her with his eyes.

Then Tom asks Grace to do the unthinkable. He asks her to stand on top of Pilgrim. Grace refuses, but Tom insists. Faltering, she puts one boot onto the horizontal animal, then the other until she is standing with her weight fully on top of him, horrified at her own necessary brutality toward her friend.

After a moment Tom helps her down.

Finally, he explains. To be lying down and helpless, in his mind, is the worst thing that could happen to Pilgrim. He goes on to elucidate that the horse needed to face his worst fears—helplessness and failure—and then see that he would be okay. To face that fear and survive would banish the last of his demons.

The story of Pilgrim and Grace and *The Horse Whisperer* illustrates what we often go through in life, and what marriage—with our spouse, with God—can teach every mate. Only when we're brought to our knees by circumstances out of our control are we able to see that we can survive. Only then do we fully see God is faithful. He gives us the strength we never thought possible, and just enough.

Then life goes on; it goes on, but we are changed, made stronger, fortified by wisdom and love.

Is it coincidence that it was "Grace" standing atop Pilgrim as he triumphed over his fears?

Possibly.

I see this as a poignant picture of God's mercy to us. His mercy is painful at times because we can't always see the purpose. But it's not only necessary. It's good—and at times a complete mystery.

In *The Horse Whisperer*, when Tom is explaining what had to happen with Pilgrim, he says, "Sometimes surrender isn't surrender at all. It's about what's going on in our hearts. About seeing clearly the way life is, and accepting it and being true to it, whatever the pain, because the pain of not being true to it is far, far greater."[4]

The beauty of being a Christian is that if we allow it, God can show us that he is even truer than our own truth, more real than our own reality.

And so the great mystery of woman, of life and circumstances, and of God becomes the great mystery of marriage. Marriage is romance and passion and love but also so much more. If there's one thing these chapters have revealed it's that there's no formula, no one way to "do" a marriage. Each of us brings our uniqueness to the union.

Also, there's this: how many facets in marriage reflect the aspects of our relationship to God and his relationship to us. This was astounding to me. I should not have been surprised, really; I think I've been taught that somewhere along the way. And God himself speaks of the parallels as he tells husbands to love their wives as Christ loved the church. But to see the expression of that on paper or as I listened to story after story was to see a miraculous unfolding of that model come to life. So many of the ideas grappled with by each of the women here draw connections back to God and our relationship with him.

Intimacy.

Submission.

Trust.

Faithfulness.

These are the ingredients of relationship as God intended. To see the beauty of the pattern laid out gives me a glimpse of the hand of God. That hand that we don't always see or look for in the routine of living, but the sight of which can move us from loss to purpose, from ordinary to enchanting.

If the expanse of ideas, seasons, and situations among the women interviewed for this project is any indication, then I think the same will be the case for those who read these pages, those who join in on these journeys. You, too, are journeying; as with the nature of journeys, you probably won't be still for very long. And as with all eventful journeys, though there are clear days, open roads, and moonlit nights, with not a soul in sight to slow you down, there are storms that blind you for a while or keep you standing still. Even a flat tire can happen. A journey is often peaceful, or seemingly long, exhilarating, full of the unanticipated, and out of control—at least our control.

Wherever you are in life's journey, be encouraged.

Men are known for being competitive, and in my experience I would say that is a common characteristic found in many of them, but women are competitive too. What is it that causes us to compare ourselves with each other? We are always sizing people up in comparison to ourselves and then judging either ourselves or others as lacking. But appearances are often deceiving. Even the one who seems the most put together has her own reality—that is, her own struggles and flaws. How I wish we all, myself included, would be more careful when we make assumptions about people's lives and judge them accordingly.

We must remember that we're each in process. We each have the messy, the mundane, and the delightful in our lives to a greater or lesser degree at one time or another. The most destructive thing we can do is envy others their triumph, rejoice in their messiness, or become discouraged by our own in relation to others'.

I have a friend who is incredibly talented—a wonderful person who is fantastically artistic, some of her work published and award winning. Her work space in her home is a sight to behold. There are shelves upon shelves, drawers, and containers full of every tool, paint, fabric, paper, or embellishment you can imagine, each having its own rightful place.

Upon seeing some of her projects for the first time, I told her that I'd always considered myself to be creative, but that in light of her remarkable talent I was now convinced I didn't have a creative bone in my body (ah, there I go with comparisons . . .)! She is so brilliant that she can take the most simple and seemingly unimpressive thing and make it unique and beautiful. A drinking straw, a piece of yarn, a torn piece of paper, a yellowed sheet of music, and an old math textbook have all been transformed into art in her hands. I would throw out an old textbook (a math one would be the first in the trash), and a piece of sheet music would be useless to me. I would see a drinking straw only for what it is—a drinking straw, never more than just that. But through her eyes she sees the potential that is there, and with her hands uses it to create beauty.

Gazing upon some of her work I was struck anew that this is what God does. God looks at the messy or the mundane or the just plain simple and uses it for beauty and for purpose. A straw is more than a straw, an old textbook more than a textbook, a man and a woman and their marriage so much more than just that. They are something precious and holy; whatever state they're in, they're seen through the eyes of an artist.

Notes

1. George Eliot, *Adam Bede* (New York: Penguin Classics, 1980), 532.

2. C. S. Lewis, *An Experiment in Criticism* (Cambridge, NY: Cambridge University Press, 1992).

3. Lorraine Ali and Lisa Miller, "The Secret Lives of Wives," July 12, 2004, http://newsweek.com.

4. Nicholas Evans, *The Horse Whisperer* (New York: Delacorte Press, 1995), 417.

acknowledgments

I am infinitely grateful to all who made this project possible, and it has been my privilege to work with so many wonderful people.

There is no question in my mind that meeting my literary agent, Tina Jacobson, was by purpose, and I am immensely grateful to her. She believed in this project from the beginning and worked in many ways to bring it about. I have the highest respect for her. My sincere thanks also goes to Jeanette Thomason, acquisitions editor at Revell. I felt an immediate connection with her at our first meeting, and I am so thankful for her vast knowledge and enthusiastic support from the beginning.

Also, my appreciation goes to my friend Robert Wolgemuth for his time, expertise, and guidance when the idea for this book was first taking shape.

My gratitude to the many women I interviewed is vast. Without them this book would not have come to fruition. I am indebted to them for their willingness to be open and authentic, and I learned from the insight of each one of them. I was touched by their love and commitment, and their words and stories remain with me.

I am so appreciative to my friends Jill Carattini and Bridget Holly, who cheered me on and shared numerous conversations together, both serious and humorous, about this subject. I am thankful for their belief in me, as well as the support of my family and husband. Lastly, to my dear sister, Naomi Zacharias, my gratitude to her is deep for reading drafts over and over so many times, giving her honest input, sharing her insight, and for always passionately believing in me even when I didn't.

Sarah Zacharias Davis is the director of marketing and events for Ravi Zacharias International Ministries. She graduated from Covenant College with a degree in education and now lives with her husband in Roswell, Georgia. This is her first book.